AFTER OCCUPY

What Next for the World?

FRANK SYKES

For book orders, email orders@traffordpublishing.com.sg

Most Trafford Singapore titles are also available at major online book retailers.

Printed in Singapore.

ISBN: 978-1-4669-9179-8 (sc)
ISBN: 978-1-4669-9180-4 (hc)
ISBN: 978-1-4669-9181-1 (e)

Library of Congress Control Number: 2013910657

Trafford rev. 06/07/2013

 www.traffordpublishing.com.sg

Singapore
toll-free: 800 101 2656 (Singapore)
Fax: 800 101 2656 (Singapore)

FOREWORD

"In this well-structured, compact, and intellectual book about supporting the majority of humanity (and the planet itself), the author has composed an extremely important work. The world indeed needs to share his thoughts and tools for action."

ACKNOWLEDGMENTS

This booklet would not have been possible without the use of the brave independent or alternative international media outlets and activists.

Over the eight years of research and writing I have read books but focused on the internet, reading some 40,000 articles. In the 'Links', pages 89-108, the internet articles of many of those media outlets are given. I am clearly indebted to the work completed by them and the excellent writing of the authors.

I am also indebted to my extremely competent and helpful editor, Adrian Doesburg, MA, Member Society of Editors and Member Institute of Professional Editors, who lives as we all should with a smile on his face.

The brilliant cartoon and design of the front cover is the work of Mark Lynch.

Frank Sykes

26 March 2013

ABOUT THE AUTHOR

Frank Sykes, BA, BEc, has had a varied working life in Australia that has included time as a lobster fisherman, senior executive officer in planning and research, tertiary lecturer, accountancy practice principal and small business consultant.

His community involvement includes being a member of Apex, sporting clubs, and being on the committees of non-profit welfare organisations.

CONTENTS

CHAPTER 1

'OCCUPY' GLOBAL ACTION FOR JUSTICE

The cost of lack of interest in public affairs
is to be ruled by evil men.
Plato (BC 427-347)

Politics is the art of preventing people from taking
part in affairs which properly concern them.
Paul Valery (1871-1945)

Who controls the food supply controls the people.
Who controls the energy can control whole continents.
Who controls money can control the world.
Attributed to Henry Kissinger (1923-)

1.1. 1% Wealth and Control[1]

The '1%', their predatory corporations—some larger than nations—
and vested interests own and control the world's resources. Their

unmerited wealth, gained often by unproductive speculation, allows them control of:

- world organisations, governments, politicians, public servants, the mainstream media, academia, and the '99%'; and
- the world's food, energy, and money.

1.2. Today's Crises[2]

Today's crises are not the result of accident or miscalculation but of the pursuit of power, crimes against humanity, greed, and the mantra of 'neoliberalism.' (See chapter 2.)

The 1% have brought about:

- the global financial crisis (GFC) (chapter 3);
- the 'real' economy or fiscal crisis (chapter 4); and
- the environmental crisis (chapter 5).

1.3. Participatory Democracy and Justice[3]

The continued global domination of the 1% will ensure continuing crises and the economic, social, cultural, and environmental collapse of nations and planet earth.

➤ Modern 'democracy' (Greek *dēmokratia* government by the people) is a sham. True democracy must be genuinely participatory at all levels of government. The 99% must demand global justice, constitutional and legislative change, and action to bring about:

- a financial and economic system that ensures sufficiency and equity for all;
- sustainability and minimum destruction of the environment; and
- a world of peace.

➤ Constitutional and legislative amendments to overcome the evil machinations of the 1% and for Participatory democracy must be voted on immediately by referendum or its equivalent.

➤ **'Occupy'** must develop a political action program and become a leading part of a globally coordinated movement of activist groups, youth, and 'elders.'

➤ To ensure that it is not hijacked and derailed, **Occupy** must:

- develop a coordinated action agenda and leadership structure with other movements and within its own troops;
- continue to be morally and actively courageous;
- enlist the morally and actively courageous among the '1%' and their vested interests to assist in its cause; and
- become financially strong.

1.4. Resistance to Change[4]

There will be massive resistance to any change: the closer the 99% and **Occupy** get to achieving their just goals, the more resistance there will be.

Occupy must be relentless in its demand for justice. United in its global billions, the 99% will succeed; divided, it will fail. For the sake of humanity, today's youth and future generations, and planet earth, it must succeed.

CHAPTER 2

SHAM DEMOCRACIES

2.1. 1%: The Enemies of Democracy[5]

The '1%,' their predatory corporations, and vested interests are the enemies of democracy and of international and national constitutions and laws. Their membership is said to include some 6,000 individuals who constitute a dominant global 'super class.' They are, in effect, a world government that controls world organisations, governments, financial institutions, other global corporations—and billions of the world's people.

The remaining 99% have been silenced by the 1% and their economic policies of neoliberalism.

2.1.1. Constitution (or Equivalent) and Legislation

➢ To bring about justice and lawful change, the 99% must first consider all existing relevant legislation, and where necessary, they must amend the constitution at every level of government:

- the requirements for constitutional amendment vary between nations, the level of government, and the subject matter; an international standard must be the goal;
- to ensure that action and legal proceedings against those suspected of fraud can get underway unhindered, it will be necessary to waive here any

    (a) statutes of limitations;
    (b) any laws of 'double jeopardy'; and
    (c) the corporate veil.

2.1.2. The Neoliberalism Mantra

The 1% has foisted neoliberalism (aka economic rationalism) upon a silenced 99% through the financing of 'think tanks,' academia, educational institutions, and the mainstream media.

Its principles rely on the following myths:

- deregulation and minimal government intervention in markets;
- 'free' trade (aka trade liberalisation);
- privatisation of the people's assets; and
- the catastrophic, never-ending pursuit of economic 'growth.'

As a result, global financial, 'real economy' (fiscal), and environmental disasters are imminent.

2.1.3. Climate of Fear

Fear, threats, and indefinite imprisonment of citizens without trial are used to silence the 99%. Fear was used by the 1% to convince us that it was essential to bail out—with taxpayers' monies—the financiers who had brought about the 2008 GFC.

Threats, legal action, and incarceration have been used against many, including the whistleblowers Bradley Manning and Julian Assange and members of the **Occupy** movement. Financial blockade has been used against WikiLeaks.

> ➢ Whistleblowers must be protected by law:

- leaks of 'secret' information from public-sector bureaucrats and others have been essential in keeping governments accountable and the 99% protected and informed;
- free legal assistance must be provided to whistleblowers; their lawyers and the people must have access to them (*habeas corpus*), including by means of 24/7 camera surveillance if imprisoned;
- organisations such as Anonymous and WikiLeaks must be adequately funded; and
- bureaucrats who ignore information for which governments should be held accountable must be penalised as culpable, anti-democratic conspirators.

2.1.4. The Surveillance State: National Security and Domestic Spying

Every nation must protect itself and its people. Global and national security systems are essential. They go under a variety of names, and presumably, many are unknown.

When used for domestic spying on a state's own citizens, they are used outside their main purpose. For example, the US National Security Agency (NSA) and its related agencies have recorded some 20 trillion communications of ordinary Americans.

➤ Under every nation's constitution and law:

- the 99% must be fully informed and given the opportunity to approve by vote the framework, cost, and powers of a government's national security and domestic spying programs;
- at minimum, the programs must comply with international agreements on data protection and privacy; and
- any use of private agencies and corporations must be approved by vote.

➤ The 99% should combat the illegal use of the 'surveillance state' by:

- becoming aware of their rights when interacting with government agencies; and
- anonymously communicating on the internet.

2.1.5. Dominance of Information Flows

Information dominance—one aspect of 'full-spectrum dominance'—is a stated policy of the United States. Propaganda, lies, misinformation, cover-ups, spin, secrecy, and information overload are part of the process that allows the 1%, their corporations, and vested interests to sideline the will of the majority and pursue their agendas undetected.

➢ Political propaganda by TV, radio, media releases, film (e.g., *Operation Hollywood*), and 'information advertisements' are used to influence opinion. The people must be given the right to decide the use of public money for partisan government propaganda.

➢ If politicians in their campaigns and public servants are found guilty of political lies, misinformation, cover-ups, and spin, they should be brought to account. Lies must be an indictable offence, and perpetrators' taxpayer-funded superannuation and other payments stopped.

➢ The 2003 invasion of Iraq was a fundamental breach of international law. The perpetrators must be brought to account:

  ▪ both the United Kingdom and Australia are parties to the UN International Criminal Court (ICC) statute—thus Tony Blair, John Howard, and their administrations must be prosecuted in the ICC;

  ▪ the United States has not ratified the statute; however, eminent US legal experts have argued that George W. Bush, Dick Cheney, and their administration could be indicted for murder.

> In the matter of the torture of prisoners, the people must be:

- provided with full information on the framework and methods used where any form of physical or psychological torture has been applied; and
- given the right to vote on all relevant legislation.

A list of 13 officials in the George W. Bush administration who made possible the torture and rendition of US political prisoners and the CIA's secret sites is available. All must be brought to justice.

> The Middle East is the subject of massive secrecy and deception, including exaggerated security threats. It has been argued that it is in Israel's best interest for the Middle East, including Israel, to be made free of nuclear, biological, and chemical weapons. This could set a pattern for similar measures to be applied throughout the world.

2.1.6. Social Engineering and Political Correctness

'Social engineering' and 'political correctness,' as used by the 1%, involve:

- political denigration and manipulation of the media and public arenas to vilify and silence those holding differing opinions; and
- buzzwords and terms such as *anti-Semitic, discrimination* (often prohibiting rightful differentiation), *inevitable,*

national interest and security, homophobia and other phobias, *progress, racist* and *terrorist.*

The term *anti-Semitic* has allowed the United States and Israel to do as they wish and continue the Palestinian holocaust.

➤ There may be little that can be done about the use of political denigration and buzzwords, other than ignoring them or legislating against their misuse.

2.2. Participatory Democracy[6]

Intermittent elections have degenerated into farcical political circuit breakers to placate the people. They do not ensure genuine participatory democracy.

➤ It is the duty of the 99% to immediately take action to regain rightful democratic control from their governments and insist on:

- an immediate review of existing constitutions and legislation to ensure that strategic political decisions are made by vote of the people or their local community representative at all levels of government—national, state/provincial and local;
- being fully informed in a timely and succinct manner;
- the prohibition of campaign funding of candidates and other political donations by corporations, and limiting those made by individuals to a legislated amount; and

- the people having the power to remove from office all elected and public officials e.g. by impeachment or a 'recall election'.

2.3. Strategic Decisions[7]

A properly informed 99% is more than capable of making strategic political decisions.

➤ In addition to other matters raised in this document, the people must be enabled to exercise their democratic right to vote on strategic decisions on the following matters:

1. War and The Judiciary (2.4)
2. World Organisations (2.5)
3. The Public Sector (2.6)
4. Corporations and Lobbyists (2.7 and 2.8)
5. Global and National Banking Systems and Financial Institutions (Chapter 3)
6. Government Revenue and Expenditure (Chapter 4)
7. Environmental Matters (Chapter 5)

2.3.1. Constitutional and Legislative Framework

➤ In cases where the accommodation or delegation by the elected government for the people to make strategic decisions is not legally possible, there must be constitutional change to make it so at every level of government.

➢ Citizen-initiated Referenda (CIRs) must be allowed to enable a public vote on matters such as:

- the making of constitutional changes;
- a 'voters' veto' to block laws passed by Parliaments or their equivalent; and
- the making of new laws by voters.

➢ The plebiscite process on the passing of strategic decisions which are not the subject of a referendum must be made possible at every level of government. To be effective, when the people's wish is established, it must be binding on government.

➢ The right of any person or organisation to petition Parliament or its equivalent to take or not to take a particular course of public policy must be unimpeded.

➢ An elected 'citizen jury' can be the prime information and opinion source on a given constitutional or legislative matter. The 'juries' would then be a platform for participatory democracy, where the electorate makes the final decision by vote.

➢ Electronic democracy ('eDemocracy') is the most efficient means of empowering citizens or their local nominees to participate in the democratic process. Modern electronic and communication 'smart' technologies must be immediately developed to ensure that the 99%:

- receive reliable, timely and succinct information;
- can participate in debate on strategic decisions; and

- as already successfully introduced throughout the world, have their votes accurately recorded by electronic voting.

➢ Video conferencing, virtual classrooms and internet communities as a forum for debate must be financed by government.

2.3.2. People Fully Informed

➢ It is the duty of taxpayer-funded politicians and public servants to timely and comprehensively inform the people of all matters relating to their strategic decisions.
➢ The bases for decision-making must be provided in one-page summaries in point form for the people's decision. Full detail must be available if requested. Inappropriate complexity of information provided should be taken as fraudulent or evidence of lack of understanding by the presenters of the 'information'

2.4. War and the Judiciary[8]

➢ War ultimately treats the 99% as 'canon fodder'. The initiation of any form of war, including the 'war on terror', unmanned aerial vehicles, land and underwater drones, and 'special services' attacks must comply with international agreements and be the subject of national vote by a properly informed people.

➤ Appointment of the judiciary at all levels and decisions on mandatory sentencing must be made by the people.

2.5. World Organisations[9]

2.5.1. General

➤ There must be true democratic decision-making processes globally.
➤ There must be a revamp of all international bodies and institutions, and review of:

- their structure and cost;
- all rights of veto, such as in the UN Security Council;
- the 'one-dollar-one-vote' principle, which favours the richest countries;
- international legislation; and
- agreements between any international organisation and nations.

➤ World organisation heads, senior officials and regulators must be appointed by vote of the people.

2.5.2. Corporate Influence

The undemocratic influence of global corporations and their lobbyists on the UN and its agencies, on the EU and other international organisations has been detrimental to international policy making and development strategies.

The UN '3 Sisters' (the World Trade Organisation (WTO), the International Monetary Fund (IMF) and the World Bank) have an overwhelming influence on international affairs. They undermine nations by favouring global corporations on matters such as tied loans to nations, privatisation of people's assets and trade liberalisation:

- corporate lobbying has demanded unfair loans and trade rules which have undermined the fight against poverty, hindered rather than helped poor countries, and has allowed corporations to violate environmental, social and human rights and labour standards; and
- public-private partnerships support corporations in opening up markets and in facilitating access to governments.

➢ By means of cooperation between all nations and the strategic decision-making available to their people:

- the WTO, IMF and World Bank must be reconstituted or replaced; and
- the influence of corporations and their lobbyists on all international organisations must be strictly regulated.

2.6. Public Sector[10]

2.6.1. Community Involvement

> ➤ The people must be empowered to exercise ongoing control over the public sector, which it 'owns', and finances at all levels of government and world organisations.
> ➤ The public sector bureaucracy must advise and inform the 99% to enable them to make strategic and major operational/administrative decisions. Policy information available to top bureaucrats must also be readily available to the electorate.
> ➤ The 99% must have ongoing power to decide on the amount and presentation of information which they require. The information provided must be timely, succinct, impartial, comprehensive and continuous.

2.6.2. Regulation

At each level of government the cost of the public sector must be determined at the time of every annual budget by vote of the relevant 99%. The number and responsibility of public sector departments should be determined simultaneously and overlap of public sector departmental activities and responsibilities avoided.

> ➤ Appointments of heads of public sector departments, regulatory authorities, agencies, advisory bodies and boards,

and of other senior public servants should be a transparent part of democracy and made by vote of the people.

➤ The public sector is rightly staffed in India by Indians, in China by Chinese, in Japan by Japanese. The staffing of the public sector should similarly be heavily weighted towards indigenous persons and those born within the country.

➤ Privatisation and Outsourcing (chapter 4)

➤ Where the public sector is responsible for managing public funds and their investment (chapter 4), the people must decide by vote on where funds are to be placed.

2.7. Corporations[11]

2.7.1. General Regulation

Predatory corporations include various large global enterprises ('multinationals', 'transnationals' (TNEs)). They have turnovers greater than the GDP of many nations and consequently have an undemocratic influence:

- they dictate the policies of governments and world institutions; and
- their directors and management have as their prime objective maximising profits for their shareholders and inflated incomes for themselves.

➤ It must be legislated, with necessary constitutional amendment, that:

- the people determine by vote the national and global regulations required to ensure national sovereignty and to control the activities of corporations, their advertising and payment to their executives;
- the people appoint all regulators responsible for the control of corporate activity;
- the directors and management of corporations have a fiduciary relationship not only to their shareholders but to the people at large; and
- corporations, directors and management be severely penalised for any financial and environmental havoc which they cause.

2.7.2. Nationalisation

➢ Consideration must be given to transferring the ownership of injurious corporations to the people, by nationalisation or cooperatives. This action has already been taken in various parts of the world.

2.7.3. Other (Chapters 3-5)

2.8. Lobbyists[12]

Lobbyists exist in all nations, and number in the many thousands. Those acting for the 1%, the finance sector, fossil fuel, nuclear and agribusiness corporations have had a severely adverse impact on the sustainability of planet earth. Politicians bound to corporations that

fund their expenses and election campaigns have encouraged fraud
in the financial sector, the devastation of our environment and lack
of action on renewable energy independence.

> Legislation must ensure that:

- all political lobbyists are registered, and their financial
  and lobbying activities, agreements and expenses fully
  disclosed to the electorate;
- any adverse impact of their activities on the democratic
  process and society is penalised; and
- public servants are released from secrecy requirements
  in relation to lobbying.

2.9. Media[13]

2.9.1. Mainstream Media

Mainstream political news and documentaries generally represent
the uttering of the 1%. Captive to their commercial advertising
and government revenue, the mainstream media steadfastly direct
attention away from the compelling issues which impact on the
sustainability of our society and environment.

Meaningless and trivial commentary, easy and lazy news, on the
'markets' (more appropriately termed 'financial casinos') and
political party politics are the norm. Wars and drone attacks receive
passive support.

➤ Where the mainstream media, rather than refusing to write or air, simply regurgitate by advertisement or article, false claims made by politicians and corporations, they must be brought to account as co-conspirators in the misrepresentations.

➤ Mainstream newspaper media no longer need to be purchased. Their internet sites can be avoided. Mainstream radio and TV need not be switched on.

2.9.2. Alternative Information Sources

Independent Media

Numerous independent media websites provide 'news' or 'blogs'. Some provide both, and more. Provided a sophisticated and reliable website is accessed, truly independent journalism and reporting will be found.

➤ The 99% must demand government funding of their chosen independent media.

Internet Democracy

➤ Ready access to the internet for all is now critical for democracy and must be part of government policy.

➤ **Occupy** should decide and negotiate which websites are to be readily accessible without charge to approved users.

> ➤ The 99% must decide which information, communication and web search technologies are to be taxpayer-funded or nationalised as part of the public domain.

2.10. Academia[14]

Many educational institutions and academic appointees are funded by corporations to promote neoliberalism and other matters that favour the 1%.

> ➤ Strict regulation by the 99% of such funding must be legislated.

CHAPTER 3

GLOBAL FINANCIAL CRISIS (GFC)

3.1. Financial Sector[15]

3.1.1. GFC

A deregulated global financial sector and markets, as advocated by neoliberalism, has for decades been a deliberate part of the global power strategy of the 1% to control the wealth and political decisions of nations.

The former US Federal Reserve chairman Alan Greenspan admitted that the 2008 GFC and 'real' economy crisis were the result of his mistaken pursuit of that neoliberal ideology during his 18-year control of US monetary policy.

The GFC continues to this day. The bankers and global corporations dictate the global financial markets and the actions of national and local governments.

Their speculative trading in shares, other financial instruments such as 'derivatives', commodities and currencies, has produced no tangible goods or services. It has merely generated intangible windfall 'paper' money gains for them at the expense of the 99%. The gains have been used to gain monopoly ownership of the world's money and to purchase 'real' economy assets in the productive economic sectors, including food and energy.

Documentaries, articles and books on the GFC and continuing financial crisis have established that there is a plethora of parasitic governments, regulators, banks, other financial institutions and credit rating agencies involved.

3.1.2. Confidence in Justice and the Financial System

Confidence in justice and the financial system must be restored.

> ➢ Coordinated global and national regulation of financial markets must be introduced and enforced to control the activities of financial sector corporations and restore national sovereignty. As the United States was the prime cause of the 2008 GFC action must commence there.
> ➢ Appropriate legislation and where necessary constitutional amendments, including waiving of the Statute of

Limitations, Double Jeopardy and the lifting of the Corporate Veil (2.1.1 above) here, must be introduced.

➤ Regulation must be drafted by public sector regulators chosen by popular vote.

➤ On rational financial, economic and ethical grounds financial sector law breakers must be brought to account.

➤ Information on all matters must be continuously updated on social and independent media websites and made required reading and viewing at schools and other educational institutions.

3.2. Global Financial Institutions and Regulations[16]

3.2.1. Global Financial System

The core international economic and financial systems were established at the 1944 Bretton Woods Conference when the 'gold standard', the International Monetary Fund (IMF), the World Bank and the World Trade Organisation (WTO) were confirmed.

In 1971 the United States unilaterally terminated convertibility of US dollars to gold and defaulted on its sovereign debt obligations. The 'gold standard' system collapsed. The US dollar became the fiat 'reserve currency' of choice, which has grossly and unfairly favoured that country.

The IMF and World Bank have imposed stringent loan conditions on recipient countries, requiring them to adopt 'deregulation', the removal of trade barriers, and a range of neoliberalist policies.

With the WTO they have actively supported global corporations whose requirements they have forced countries to accept. Together they encroach on national sovereignty and have contributed to the current world crises.

3.2.2. Reform Needed: Systemic Reform

➤ Reputable experts recommend immediate global systemic reforms under a new international agreement that replaces the IMF, World Bank and US$ reserve currency:

- integrated international and national finance systems and regulations under a global financial regulatory authority such as a UN 'Global Economic Coordination Council'; the authority must regulate the 'shadow banking system', including hedge funds (below), money market funds and structured investment vehicles;
- a new global reserve system and currency with links to gold, and an updated version of Professor John Maynard Keynes' 1944 global bank, which would issue its own global currency convertible into national currencies at fixed rates of exchange;
- capital controls and the setting of all interest rates, including the interbank lending rate (the 'Libor') and other lender rates, under a global regulatory authority;
- a global credit ratings system which ensures that all assets and liabilities of financial institutions are valued and fully disclosed to an internationally approved and readily understood standard;

- legal restrictions on the leverage/gearing of financial institutions, and a maximum debt-equity ratio;
- global anti-money laundering standards which ensure that the movement of 'sovereign wealth funds' and other monies across national borders is controlled and immediately reported;
- the prohibition of 'offshore' tax havens;
- strict regulation of corporate financial institutions, private investment funds, equity funds and hedge funds;
- the banning of innovative financial products and derivatives unless compliant with strict regulations;
- the dismantling of megabanks; and
- regulation of the salaries and remuneration of executives of banks, financial institutions and other entities in the financial sector.

➢ Reforms must embrace such matters as:

- host country sovereignty and more stable and sustainable development finance;
- regulation of foreign subsidiaries;
- mechanisms for handling sovereign debt restructuring and cross-border investment disputes;
- foreign investment, ownership and control (chapter 4); and
- tax enforcement and collection of taxes relating to 'free' trade and foreign investment transactions (see chapter 4).

➢ All reforms and appointments of the global bank CEO and all global regulators must be approved by vote of the nations' people or their nominees. No government, entity, or individual should have veto powers.

➤ Failure to comply with any regulation must incur:

- for corporation and owners, takeover of their assets by government; and
- for directors and management, a substantial jail term and immediate surrender to the people of all assets directly and indirectly owned by them.

3.2.3. Derivatives

The grandiose term 'derivative' includes concocted and deliberately complex financial instruments and fraudulent 'securities' of colossal amounts of 'money'. Their underlying assets have included toxic sub-prime mortgages. They are generally divorced from reality and worthless to all but the 1% and their vastly overpaid financiers and 'quants', the masters of financial modeling and automated 'algorithmic' trading on the financial markets.

Having played a major role in the 2008 GFC, the global holdings of derivatives were estimated to be $1.4 quadrillion ($1400,000,000,000,000) by 2012, truly a weapon of worldwide mass destruction. The largest US banks—Goldman Sachs, Bank of America, Citibank and JPMorgan Chase—were exposed to hundreds of trillions of derivatives. They, banks of all nations, and others were vulnerable to the inevitability of the next financial and fiscal crisis.

Yet eminent opponents of derivatives—such as Brooksley Born and Elizabeth Warren in the US—were denigrated and ignored.

➤ Action on derivatives must be immediately taken:

- ban or strictly regulate them as recommended by the vast majority of independent experts;
- compel all 'Over the Counter' (OTC) derivatives, estimated to make up the bulk of the market, to be cleared through central clearing houses, and to be traded on separate regulated exchanges;
- levy a financial transactions tax (FTT) at punitive rates on all derivatives trading or
- nationalise all concocted derivatives at the true value of their underlying tangible assets under the control of an international regulator.

➤ Before being put onto markets, derivatives and other novel financial instruments must be approved by the people and their chosen independent experts.

3.3. National Financial Institutions[17]

3.3.1. Banks

Fractional Reserve Banking

Our 'money', whether a piece of paper, coin or electronic equivalent, is 'fiat' money, no longer backed by gold but only by the relevant government.

Throughout the world 'fractional reserve banking' has allowed private banks to 'create' money 'out of thin air', by lending more than they have to keep on hand or on deposit at their Reserve Bank. It has become a tool for control by the 1% and was a major contributor to the GFC.

> For justice and for people control of their economies, the only permanent solution is to immediately amend Constitutions and/or legislate:

- that Reserve Banks alone have the power to create money, subject to approval by vote of the people;
- to remove the ability of private banks to create money and debt;
- that the funds used to bailout a country to overcome its sovereign debt problems are not credited to that country's private banks but to public 'people's banks';
- to severely modify the government policy 'of inflation targeting' which provides a cover for keeping interest rates high, thus benefiting lenders but not debtors; and
- to audit the books of all banks to identify hidden 'toxic waste'.

3.3.2. Separate Retail from Investment Banking

> The 'retail' business of banks must be confined by regulation to the provision of a safe place for deposits, secured loans to individuals for housing and other safe loans to individuals and business:

- retail banking must be split from 'merchant', insurance and 'investment' banking;
- financial institutions such as people's banks, community development banks and credit unions must be restricted to 'retail' banking; and
- government guarantees should be confined to retail banks.

'Too Big to Fail' a Fallacy

➤ If private banks decide to merge and consolidate for economies of scale and to boost profits, bailout by the taxpayer is unwarranted and should not be undertaken.

3.3.3. 'People's Banks'

➤ The 'localisation' of people-owned or cooperative retail banks is essential to encourage and support local economic development and trading with local business.

➤ Such banks or government retail banks should be conveniently located e.g. close to Post Offices and government Tax Offices.

➤ Individuals should move their deposits and debt to those banks and demand that their local institutions use those banks.

3.4. Bring to Account Those Responsible for GFC[18]

3.4.1. Matters

➢ Immediate investigation of the fraudulent money trail and action to recover stolen monies are essential:

  ■ in the derivative, financial, commodity and exchange markets; and
  ■ from the markets to tax havens and to investment or purchase of equity in the 'real' economy.

➢ By constitutional amendment and legislation if required:

  ■ institutional and individual immunity from damages for fraud must be prohibited; waiving of the Statute of Limitations, Double Jeopardy, and the Corporate Veil (2.1.1 above) must be introduced;
  ■ all settlements by regulators must be reviewed for further action by the people's chosen representatives;
  ■ any taxpayer-funded bailout monies paid by governments must immediately be repaid in full to the people and those responsible for the bailouts brought to account; and
  ■ steps must immediately be taken globally to freeze and hold in trust for the people all assets, whether corporate, trust or individual that are suspected on reasonable grounds of having been fraudulently acquired, until all suits have been resolved.

3.4.2. Some of Those Responsible for GFC

Central Banks and Regulators

The US Federal Reserve is a concoction of private Federal Reserve Banks. Former Goldman Sachs employees and other contributors to the GFC are employed by or closely related to it.

> ➤ Reserve Banks and regulators must be independent of corporations. They must be public institutions and their members chosen by vote of the people. They must be made to disclose full details of all assistance, including government loans provided at below-market rates to private financial institutions.
> ➤ In the US, Greenspan, Paulson and Bernanke are examples of regulators that are candidates for swift legal action. It was Alan Greenspan who, together with Arthur Levitt and Robert Rubin, stopped Brooksley Born (Chair of the US Commodity Futures Trading Commission) from imposing regulations on derivatives.

Corporate Criminals

> ➤ Though a handful of suits have generated settlements, the penalties imposed on corporate financial sector criminals have been inadequate. Justice will not be done unless the directors, CEOs and loan officers at the heart of the GFC are brought to account. If found guilty, they should be stripped of their fraudulently acquired assets and jailed.

Credit Rating Agencies

Credit rating has been outsourced to private credit ratings agencies and enshrined in regulation. The ratings determine the interest rates for national government bonds. Fraudulently or otherwise, they did not foresee the 2008 GFC and conferred AAA status onto worthless assets. Yet they continue to issue credit ratings to this day.

> ➤ They must be held liable for their incorrect ratings proven by the GFC and shut down.
> ➤ Legislation must ensure that new credit rating agencies are nationalised and their ratings independently verified, e.g. by a UN 'Global Economic Coordination Council' (3.2.2).

Hedge Funds

'Hedge funds' deal in highly speculative 'investments', such as derivatives. Prosecutions suggest that many trade in any way which they can find, whether legal or not, and pay exorbitant performance fees to their managers.

> ➤ A handful has been prosecuted. If the identities of fraudulent funds and their management are known they must be brought to justice.
> ➤ Hedge funds must be globally outlawed, or strictly and independently regulated or taxed on all transactions and income at prohibitive rates.

Financial Planners/Advisers/Managers etc

Many of the world's financial sector 'experts' (financial planners/ managers/strategists etc) have been exposed as charlatans involved in short-term speculation. They generally earn their income without any consequence for bad advice. It is in their financial interest to turn over their clients' investment portfolios as often as possible.

Burton Malkiel claimed that "an investment portfolio chosen by a blindfolded monkey throwing darts at a newspaper's financial pages would do just as well as one carefully selected by the experts". The Wall Street Journal's Dartboard Contest has been unable to satisfactorily dispute the claim.

- Pension funds must be in the hands of public bodies chosen by the vote of the relevant electorate.
- Legislation should ensure that the investment of other funds of the 99% should be taken out of the hands of 'experts' in the private sector, unless:

  - their investments are subject to strict regulation, comply with the UN principles for responsible investment (UN PRI), 'environmental, social and governance' (ESG) matters and 'socially responsible investing' (SRI) as determined by the vote of the people;
  - any payment to them by a client is on a 'fee for service' based on time; and
  - all advice is subject to a legally binding warranty or guarantee.

Mainstream Media

In its reporting on the financial markets/casinos, the mainstream media regurgitates meaningless jargon provided by its 'experts':

- exaggerated inevitable and miniscule 'point' and 'percent' movements on the world's financial markets, and simplistic explanations of them; and
- simplistic 'forecasts'.

By such reporting, the 99% have been convinced to entrust hard-earned monies to many financial sector fraudsters. 'Market values' are artificially boosted by the continuous investment of such funds.

➢ The 99% must be regularly provided with the advice of independent expert media chosen by the people, e.g. the US Weiss Inc.

3.4.3. Parasites and Criminals Identified

➢ Action must be taken against those corporations and individuals already identified as having fraudulently acquired their obscene wealth: e.g.,

- 2009: 'Subprime Top 25' lenders of whom 20 "closed, stopped lending, or were sold to avoid bankruptcy".
- 2010: 10 most corrupt capitalists in the US economy, which included the 'Goldman D.C. Army'. At least 48 former employees of Goldman Sachs have been at the highest reaches of political power around the world.

- 2011: 9 Wall Street executives who profited from the boom and bust.

➢ The procedure known as 'securitisation' was a major contributor to the GFC. It encouraged reckless lending and hid risky home loans. Their lenders must be prosecuted where they have:

- attempted to foreclose on properties which they didn't own; and/or
- a potentially massive liability for non-payment of mortgage filing fees.

3.5. Taxation[19]

3.5.1. General

➢ Tax law must allow government acting for the people to:

- waive any Statute of Limitations, Double Jeopardy and the Corporate Veil (2.1.1 above);
- immediately freeze assets of reasonably suspected tax evaders;
- use 'default assessments' which place the onus of proof on a tax evader;
- ensure that there are personal consequences for company directors, management and shareholders of a corporate tax evader; and
- institute criminal proceedings to jail tax evaders.

3.5.2. FTT—1972 Tobin Tax

> A financial transactions tax (FTT) must be levied not only on international currency transactions, but on all other financial trades. The advantages of an all-embracing FTT include:

- speculative and fraudulent high frequency trading is discouraged;
- destabilising currency and commodity market speculation is discouraged;
- revenue is generated for expenditure on social services, public health, public infrastructure, sustainable energy and climate improvement programs; and
- it could be administered by a UN body (3.2.2).

3.5.3. Finance Industry Bonuses

> Any bonuses paid to executives and employees by the bailout recipients (3.4.1), whether prior—or post-2008 GFC, must be immediately repaid to the relevant government.
> All future bonuses should be taxed at punitive rates.

3.5.4. Tax Havens and Offshore Profits

> International action must be taken to end the use of tax havens and transfer of profits offshore. It must be policed by a UN entity (3.2.2), with the legal authority to insist on

full disclosure and the power to collect any tax evaded e.g. by 'default assessment'.

3.5.5. Individual Tax Rates

Present taxation is based on the 'trickle down' myth: when the wealthiest prosper, the less wealthy will also prosper. Yet the wealth increase for the 1% rich has been far greater than that for the 99%.

After WWII individual tax rates on the top income earners of recovering nations were globally much higher than today: e.g. 91-92% in the United States.

➢ To recover from our present crises and in the interest of justice, democracy and progress it is essential to immediately return to the post WWII tax rates.
➢ Capital and income tax rates should be weighted heavily on the rich—defined as those with family earnings or capital assets at a level of triple the national average.

3.5.6. Other Corporate

Two-thirds of US corporations paid no taxes in 1998-2005. Others, such as Goldman Sachs, have paid an effective tax rate over time as low as 1% p.a.

➢ Corporate tax rates and tax avoidance, e.g. by the use of tax havens (3.5.4 above), must be a matter for global legislation.

CHAPTER 4

'REAL' ECONOMY CRISIS

4.1. 'Real' Economy[20]

4.1.1. Genuine Economic Activity

The 'real' (fiscal) economy involves:

- government expenditure and taxation;
- private sector investment in necessary goods and services and their production, trade, and consumer spending on such goods and services, and employment.

4.1.2. 'Real' Economy (Fiscal) Crisis

The myths of neoliberalism (2.1.2) allow the 1% to deprive countries of the capacity to manage their own economies. Its simplistic 'free market' economics:

- has ignored:

  (a) the interests of the 99% and the undemocratic activities of the 1% and its global corporations;
  (b) social and environmental considerations and indirect costs such as air pollution and devastated ecosystems caused by burning fossil fuels; and
  (c) unsustainable debt levels;

- guarantees:

  (a) an undemocratic gap between rich and poor; and
  (b) government austerity measures as opposed to proper and equitable taxation of high income earners.

To support such economics, the 1% have converted 'real' economics into an ideology which depends on mythical mathematics and tweaked financial and economic modelling.

The current crises are the inevitable result of such modelling and the greatest-ever failure of *laissez-faire*—leave-it-to-the market—economics. Reliable experts assert that unless fundamental changes are made a far more serious and long-term global fiscal crisis is inevitable.

> ➤ The prime objectives of economics in democracies, whether in dealing with the 'real' economy, financial sector, or environment, must be justice and 'the common good'. Both are minimised by neoliberalism, unfettered free markets, supremacy of self interest and profit, greed and disdain for the natural environment.

4.2. Economic Growth v Sustainability[21]

4.2.1. GDP Mantra

GDP and its numerous variants are enthusiastically manipulated by 'economists' overwhelmed by dubious 'models'. Yet their inferred estimates of a nation's level of economic activity, its 'standard of living' and 'economic growth' assume that all economic activity and growth is good:

- it includes a number of characteristics of *un*economic growth

  (a) the activities of the finance industry while 'playing in their casinos';
  (b) excessive consumption encouraged by advertising unnecessary manufactured consumer goods;
  (c) the impact of rising debt levels, government and domestic;
  (d) expenditure on unnecessary or substandard infrastructure;
  (e) massive spending on defence, including 'Wars on Terror' to satisfy the 1%'s global armament industry;
  (f) the costs of natural disasters, accidents, and family and social breakdown, including crime;
  (g) global environmental degradation and wasteful packaging.

- it ignores

  (a) human well-being, and inequalities in income;

(b) undesirable urbanisation and agribusiness (Chapter 5), the associated pollution, resource depletion, biodiversity loss and climate change;

(c) unsustainable population growth.

4.2.2. Economic Development

Reputable economists argue that the use of GDP is dangerously irrelevant. More than 1.4 billion people around the world live on less than $1.25 a day. In the US, considered to be one of the world's advanced economies, the result of GDP growth has been a record nearly 50 million Americans facing hunger in 2012, and massive environmental degradation.

➤ No longer can the 1% cause us to be embroiled in a lemming-like and relentless stampede in the pursuit of unsustainable GDP growth and an impossible Utopia. Economic 'success' must include sustainable economic growth which:

- requires economic data and measurement that differentiates between quality and quantity of growth;
- focuses on sustainable 'economic development' which meets people's needs, and which ensures a better quality of life for all, including future generations.

➤ In general terms, such economic development requires government policies that emphasise social justice and economic welfare for all, full employment, price stability, an increase in literacy, life expectancy, and leisure time, and reduced environmental degradation.

➢ The concepts of 'green growth', 'low-carbon growth' and 'green development' indicate that environmental protection and reduction of the human carbon footprint and emissions need not be at the expense of sustainable growth, but contribute to it.

➢ The rational policy for the governments of the rich world is now to keep economic growth, however measured, as close to zero as possible.

4.3. Government Revenue & Expenditure[22]

4.3.1. Budgets

➢ Under the constitution, the annual budgets of government, departments, agencies and authorities must be the subject of a vote by an informed people. They must include payments for services and functions outsourced to the private sector.

➢ If due to change of circumstances the people so demand, their budget vote must be more frequent.

➢ The vote must consider the burden of government debt on the young and on future generations, and that:

- it is unacceptable to generate *budget surpluses*, reduce deficits or repay government debt by the disposal of government-owned assets except to people-approved cooperatives;

- *budget deficits* are acceptable if used to finance public investment in infrastructure and capital goods, wholly owned by the people, that will generate future income sufficient to repay any debt incurred by the investment; but they are unacceptable to finance recurring government revenue expenditure or tax cuts.

4.3.2. Government Revenue

The principle that austerity measures are essential is absurd when corporate and individual tax rates favour the 1% and 'trickle down' will never occur.

➤ Government revenue must be increased by:

- raising individual, corporate and trust tax rates to post WWII levels (3.3.5);
- taxing unearned income from capital gains, interest, dividends, and rents at least to the same level as earned income or profit; and
- raising selected consumption taxes, tariffs, duties, and levies such as a financial transaction tax (FTT).

4.3.3. Government Expenditure

➤ Throughout a year, expenditure of taxpayers' monies above a given annual dollar figure or % of the budget must be approved by peoples' vote.

- Government and statutory authority investment, including pension funds, must follow best practice by:

  - appropriate investment in people-owned utilities such as health, water, renewable energy and its infrastructure, rail and bicycle paths, and in local manufacturing of environmentally friendly and renewable energy products; and
  - incorporating environmental, social and governance issues into decision-making.

- Governments must ensure an adequate supply of public housing by building and by:

  - ensuring tax systems, such as capital gains taxes, stamp duties and negative gearing do not reward speculation in the residential housing market; and
  - establishing 'sell and rent back' funds, managed by public housing authorities, to enable owners to sell their houses to government and rent them back at fair prices.

- The commons, national parks, rain forests and marine reserves are the 'fountains of life' and must never be diminished in size, must be owned by the people, funded by government and paid for in part by users e.g. by road tolls.
- Government expenditure, including payments to private contractors, on war, the military and its bases must be subject to vote by the people.

➤ Government expenditure on national and domestic security and the 'War on Terror' must be subject to vote by an informed people.

4.4. Individual Debt[23]

Individuals are enslaved in debt by the 1% and seduced by its advertising into consumption beyond means.

➤ Debt must be sustainable, its repayment out of earnings, not further borrowings. Savings must once again be promoted as a virtue and basis for 'real' economy expansion.
➤ The artificial manufacture of consumer needs by advertising requires strict regulation particularly in cases where it relates to:

   ▪ the advertisement target—the use of children in advertisements must be banned;
   ▪ the level of credit and repayment as a % of borrower's income; or
   ▪ the time allowed for debt repayment.

➤ Residential housing loans must be strictly regulated and based on accurate appraisals, adequate deposits (e.g. 25%) and the borrower's capacity to repay (e.g. no more than 25% of income).
➤ Legal restrictions must apply to 'reverse' mortgages, which allow the owner to borrow a portion of the estimated future value of their home without regular repayment.

4.5. Global Deregulation (Economic Globalisation)[24]

4.5.1. Impact

Economic globalisation has led to the deregulating of global relationships between nations:

- deregulation of the financial sector (Chapter 3: GFC) and capital flows, where all foreign exchange, finance and investment controls are minimised; and
- 'free' trade (aka 'trade liberalisation')—where international trade barriers, import quotas and tariffs are abolished.

Foreign Investment, Ownership & Control

Barriers to foreign investment are discouraged by the WTO. Although generally unwanted by the people, such deregulation has increased dramatically in all economic sectors, including resource, real estate, primary production, manufacturing, finance and retail:

- currency speculation and massive capital inflows into nations have allowed corporations, banks and other financial entities to become some of the largest economic entities in the world;
- local businesses, when seen to have a competitive market edge, are eliminated by foreign takeover with the result that skills, knowledge and technology are transferred to foreign corporations; and

- the enforcement of tax laws is made difficult to administer and the global tax base has been substantially diminished.

'Free' Trade Not 'Fair' Trade

'Free trade', aka 'trade liberalisation', requires nations to surrender their trade policies to the WTO requirements which are:

- trade must be the subject of minimum government regulation and barriers; and
- subsidies by governments to their producers must be minimised.

It is not 'fair' trade and has no positive economic, social or environmental outcomes:

- import and export-oriented economies, marine carbon-based transport, packaging and agribusiness have had a negative impact on land, oceans and carbon emissions (chapter 5).
- cheap labour in 'developing' nations, brutalised by long hours of work and inadequate wages, has reduced jobs and wages in 'developed' countries;
- public utilities and assets built up by communities over generations have been privatised at considerable cost to the taxpayer; and
- in the name of 'efficiency', rural communities have lost basic services and small farmers have been forced off the land.

Such 'free trade' has ensured that the winners in the global economy are global corporations. By 2006, the world's largest 500 corporations controlled some 70% of world trade; 80% of world grain production was distributed by two corporations.

4.5.2. Action

Economic globalisation, foreign investment and 'free' trade have been disastrous for communities throughout the world:

- a world without borders is ruled by unelected banks and global corporations;
- nations have lost control and ownership of their economic affairs, social structures, natural resources and environments;
- predicted benefits for 'developing' countries have proved false;
- the gap between rich and poor has widened—the 1% benefited, the 99% lost; and
- local markets, cultures and the environment have been devastated.

➢ Values and practices must immediately be adopted to produce sustainable and democratic economic systems. Nations throughout the world are being urged to abandon their commitment to deregulation and to protect their failing industries:

- trade must be 'fair' and the principle of 'free' trade abolished; and

- to ensure national sovereignty, nations must once again be permitted to decide on the barriers which they place on capital and trade flows, including quotas, tariffs and subsidies to national industries, which already exist in many nations.

➤ An FTT (3.5.2) on all transactions related to foreign investment and trade must be levied in addition to other taxes.

➤ A tax on resource extraction by foreign investors must be levied.

➤ Foreign ownership or control of the following national assets must be minimised, prohibited or, if too late, nationalised:

- strategic businesses and industries in the defence, resource and energy, manufacturing, agricultural, finance and retail sectors;
- agricultural and residential real estate; and
- management of national superannuation and pension funds.

➤ Other recommended reforms involve strict regulation of global corporations, the restoration of national sovereignty and local empowerment. They include:

- the enforcement of international regulations to curb the domination of multinational corporations and restore national sovereignty;
- prioritisation of energy, food, ecological, population, environmental and social sustainability;
- cooperation and national cooperative ownership;

- social equity and 'sufficiency' for all rather than the surplus consumption and inequitable wealth of the 1%;
- preservation of the 'commons', and fair allocation of global resources between nations and within nations (also chapter 5);
- localisation (4.6.2) and national and local boundaries, physical and economic;
- global focus on the needs of the world's poorest countries;
- international action against illegal commerce, money laundering, transnational crime and 'trafficking' in forced labour; and
- the implicit need for global grassroots movements, such as **Occupy** and the 99%.

4.6. Domestic Deregulation[25]

4.6.1. Impact

Manufacturing, Primary Production and Retail Annihilated

Domestic deregulation, competition policy and privatisation have led to a collapse of locally owned manufacturing and primary production in many countries. Corporate supermarkets, franchises and fuel outlets have taken over local retail trade.

Workforce & Wages

Global corporations compete internationally to find the cheapest labour and the most lax labour regulations:

- in both 'developed' and 'underdeveloped' nations, families are working for a record number of hours, yet living standards for workers are declining;
- in 'developed' nations:

    (a) underemployment and 'shift' labour is rife;
    (b) governments have not properly invested in education and training;
    (c) workers are replaced by migrant cheap labour;
    (d) international 'students' form a low paid workforce that have every intention of residing permanently and sponsoring family and relatives as permanent residents;
    (e) clothing industry workers are often forced to work at home for long hours at minimum wages.

Privatisation: Benefits Non-existent

Functions and services rightly considered to be essential public services and the core business of government have been privatised. The process includes:

- transfer by sale of full or partial ownership to the private sector of communication, water, gas and electricity utilities, and of financial institutions;

- transfer or 'outsourcing' to the private sector of law enforcement, prisons, defence and military matters, domestic security, welfare and social security, the collection of government revenue, labour hire arrangements, and consultancy work;
- contracting out the delivery of services previously done in-house, such as catering, printing, payroll processing, security and training.

Such privatisation, public/private partnerships (PPPs) and their variants have proved costly for the taxpayer:

- there has been corruption of public officials who make the decisions, transferring to corporations fixed assets and guaranteed income streams at base prices;
- the quality of function or service has generally fallen dramatically;
- corporations are generally bailed out by the taxpayer if they fail; and
- employment levels and apprenticeships have been substantially reduced.

4.6.2. Action

The required reforms include:

➤ Strategic national industries:

- foster the manufacture of products which ensure many desirable jobs or have potentially high-value: e.g.

motor vehicle, ship and airplane, electrical machinery, chemicals, computer equipment and nanotechnology;

- shift less skilled manufacturing and assembly overseas; and
- foster service industries, such as design, software development and higher education.

➢ Migrant labour:

- assess the social and dollar costs of acquiring skilled migrants versus the long-term benefits of educating and training a nation's people; and
- replace migrant labour with locally trained labour.

➢ Privatisation:

- end privatisation and the sale of the people's assets unless the particular proposal is put to the vote of the people and ensuring that:

  (a) any proceeds from the sale of the people's assets is used to acquire other assets (including infrastructure) capable of producing equivalent services or net income streams for the taxpayer;

  (b) the people are never excluded from essential public resources and services; and

  (c) nationalisation of privatised entities must be made possible by a people's vote.

➢ Localisation involves decentralisation and emphasis on the power of the local economy and government. It is imperative that:

- nations must satisfy their most fundamental needs, and be self-sufficient at the smallest local level, by supporting the rapid development of smaller, durable, human-orientated, localized and decentralized economies and systems which are self-sustaining;
- as part of 'grassroots' democracy, decisions and action must be taken as closely as possible by the citizen at the regional and local 'community' level;
- control over food, housing, energy, manufacturing, agriculture and national livelihoods must come from local resources, rather than depend on long distance trade which has led to insecurity and exploitation, and empowered corporate monopolies;
- a cooperative and supportive form of internationalism must ensure a global flow of technologies, information, culture, money and goods in order to protect and rebuild national and local economies;
- environmentally friendly and efficient national urban and rural systems must be maximised (chapter 5);
- the promotion of independent small businesses through mutual support and community education must be regulated, so that they outperform the megastores and 'chains'—as they have done in many localities;
- small-scale simple living values and vocational training in manual skills must be emphasised; and
- individuals must contribute to the local economy by managing with less, sharing more, and putting people, small business, the community and the planet first.

➢ Cooperation ensures the best outcome for all:

- 'cooperatives' and similar forms of worker ownership must be promoted; and
- agriculture must be de-industrialised (chapter 5 'agribusiness').

4.7. Population[26]

4.7.1. Impact

Population growth increases the human 'footprint' and environmental damage by increasing the demand for:

- infrastructure for roads, schools, hospitals, electricity and telecommunications;
- housing and land;
- food, water and sanitation systems; and
- natural resources.

Experts are convinced that solutions to the current crises are impossible without tackling the population issue at a global and national level. The rights of a nation's people must be given precedence over individual rights.

4.7.2. Peoples' Vote

➢ An informed people must immediately decide on their future national population levels within the framework of a global target:

- national border management programs including 'e-Border' to target illegal immigrants must be adequate;
- the right to vote on national population growth (by natural increase, genuine refugee intake, and permanent and temporary migration) must be weighted in favour of those born in the country and with the longest permanent residence;
- child 'benefits' must be limited to parents with a maximum of two children, and disallowed, along with social security and unemployment benefits, to new arrivals;
- future expenditure by the public sector and social engineers on the multiculturalism experiment must be agreed.

➢ Encourage public discussion on proposals to charge a 'baby levy' of say, $5,000 and an annual 'carbon tax' of up to $800 per child for families with more than two children.

CHAPTER 5

ENVIRONMENTAL CRISIS

5.1. Pollution and Climate Change[27]

5.1.1. Environmental Vandalism

The environmental crisis involves the devastating physical pollution of planet earth's natural environment and the contribution to climate change by humans: our theft of the future from today's youth and from future generations.

The 1% and vested interests bear prime responsibility:

- world organisations, governments, regulators and public servants, paid by the people and with an obligation to act in their interest, instead advance the interests of the 1%;
- the 1%'s corporations and bankers have 'captured' regulators and public servants, and are a major political barrier to minimising environmental damage and transition to clean energy;

- corporate driven supermarket and residential developments are environmentally disastrous; and
- the 1% finance academia, 'think-tanks' and a sycophantic mainstream media which foster neoliberalism and environmental pollution, and dispute the fact of human contribution to climate change.

5.1.2. Action

Immediate action to preserve and ensure an equitable and sustainable planet earth will ultimately be far less costly than inaction.

Information

➢ The 99% must be properly informed. Accurate, complete and immediate information must be made freely available by government, so that societies can reset their values, attitudes and goals towards pollution and climate change and immediately take appropriate action.

➢ People-chosen independent media and environmental activist websites must be organised into a cohesive and cooperative group, financed either by government in lieu of subsidies to corporate polluters or by tax deductible donations.

Legally Enforceable Rights of Nature

- ➤ Global recognition of the legal rights of nature and the fundamental and inalienable right of natural communities and ecosystems to exist and flourish is essential.
- ➤ Constitutional amendments and legislation must ensure that any human activity having a major deleterious effect on the environment be prohibited unless approved by an informed electorate.
- ➤ Technologies must be environmentally friendly and comply with the 'precautionary principle'. There must be:

  - measures that warn against and prevent serious risks or damage to the environment or human health; and
  - policy to prohibit or restrict the use of a product or process where there is significant scientific uncertainty about potential for environmental or health harm.

- ➤ Justice demands that the polluter must pay:

  - polluters and carbon emitters and their associated vested interests must under both national and international law be liable for past and continuing pollution and for carbon emissions;
  - the victims of pollution and climate change must receive full compensation, including restoration and reparation for the loss of land and livelihoods; and
  - a refundable levy on corporate activities with the potential to be environmentally damaging must be raised and deposited in a global people's bank.

5.2. Pollution[28]

The pollution of our planet is often hidden in faraway places. Some is invisible to the naked eye, such as the increasing 'toxicity' of the air we breathe, and of what we eat and drink and absorb through our skins.

5.2.1. Oceans

Plastics and Other Human Waste

Plastic and other human garbage float, and are absorbed in, the Pacific (the Pacific Garbage Patch), Atlantic and Indian oceans. Such waste has a deadly impact on ocean eco-systems and marine life.

We are all partially responsible if we discard goods and plastics that end up in the ocean. But global corporations that manufacture plastics and lack of government regulations are primarily to blame.

➤ The manufacturers of plastics and other waste material must be compelled to produce products that are totally biodegradable within a legal maximum number of years.
➤ The manufacturers of the plastic waste materials in the oceans must be identified and made to remove their debris from the oceans and recycle it in a biodegradable form.

Coral Reefs: Ocean Acidification

➢ Warm—and cold-water coral reefs, the marine equivalent of tropical rainforests, are essential habitats for thousands of species of plants and animals:

- they grow very slowly and must be protected;
- discharges from ships that contribute to ocean acidification and kill coral must be regulated and penalised to ensure that environmentally benign systems are used.

Ecosystem Destruction

➢ The oceans' eco-systems and animals are being devastated by destructive techniques of 'forage fishing', illegal fishing and ocean fish farming. If the situation continues, fish populations will disappear worldwide:

- 'bottom trawling' and other destructive fishing techniques must be banned;
- 'forage fish' should feed people rather than being used as animal feed;
- illegal fishing must be severely penalised; and
- ocean fish farming establishments must be approved by vote of the people.

Man-made Noise

> ➤ Man-made noise severely affects and can kill whales, dolphins and other marine life. Action must be taken to prevent the use of underwater sonar and explosives.

5.2.2. Freshwater

Demand for Water

Water supplies are near their limits in many countries:

- demand is driven by population growth, rising living standards and energy demand, rapid urbanisation and agribusiness;
- supply is hampered by deforestation, pollution, waste and climate change;
- ever more dams, built for corporate interests, have a disastrous impact on the natural environment;
- underground water sources, which often are not replenished for thousands of years, have been overused and are at critically low levels; and
- there is an ever-increasing likelihood of conflict over water between countries, regions, and urban and rural users.

> ➤ A collective response by the whole international community is needed to tackle the water resource issue. The goal

must be that clean, affordable, and safe drinking water is available to all.

> Every community must fight water polluters and inequality in the distribution of water, and promote greener solutions to water management:

- international constitutions and law must recognise the human right to clean freshwater at an acceptable cost, and guarantee that rivers, estuaries, basins and waterways are protected from degradation;
- aquifers must be given special protection;
- corporate and other freshwater polluters must be severely penalised;
- privatisation of the water supply must be abolished, as water is part of the 'commons' belonging to the people;
- solar water disinfecting and other means of purification must be provided to developing countries;
- technical knowledge, such as hydrological modelling, satellite data and irrigation control must be made available to all nations;
- infrastructure must be adequate and financed by:

  (a) rates on a tiered basis: the greater the usage, the greater the rate;
  (b) taxing industries which dispose of waste into the water supply; and
  (c) low-interest government loans to communities to ensure that special infrastructure requirements are met.

- to minimise water consumption, encouragement by government subsidy or otherwise must be given to:

  (a) appropriate urban design, e.g. permeable pavements;
  (b) decentralised wastewater recycling in city and small town areas;
  (c) investment in recycling 'grey' water and the harvesting of rain (e.g. by rainwater tanks) and storm water; and
  (d) water-wise homes by appropriate water pricing and restrictions.

5.2.3. Deforestation and Land Clearing

The decades-long destruction of the planet's rain forests for building, paper, palm plantation and energy has been relentless:

- over half of the world's rain forests have been cut down;
- food and water sources, flora, animal species, cultural sites and artifacts have been contaminated or destroyed;
- corporations have been involved in widespread human rights abuses, political corruption and the brutal suppression of opponents.

Land has been rapidly degraded, by population growth, grazing animals, agribusiness, and fossil-fuel extraction. Deserts grow.

  ➤ Environmentally damaging deforestation and land clearing practices, and the associated crimes of human rights abuse and political corruption must be made criminal offences and punitive fines imposed.

5.2.4. Energy Mining and Power Plants

> - The people must know the source by location, extraction and processing of energy they use.
> - Resource taxes must be levied for the extraction and use of finite resources and associated pollution.
> - Polluters must be compelled to clean up and restore extraction sites as nearly as possible to their previous condition.

Coal

Governments divert taxpayers' funds to finance research into 'clean coal' and carbon capture and storage (CCS). The pursuit of 'clean coal' by whatever means is a false solution to the global energy and environmental crises:

- coal will never be 'clean'—it causes pollution when mining it, cleaning it, disposing of waste, transporting it, and building its infrastructure; coal-fired power plants are the largest source of man-made carbon dioxide emissions;
- coal is not 'safe'—there are known hazards for miners, and its production increases chronic local illnesses;

- coal is not 'cheap'—the true costs of its environmental devastation add billions of dollars to its published corporate costs and price;
- coal is detrimental, not 'good', for the economy.

➢ Investment in renewable solar and wind power is far more energy-efficient (5.3.5): it can produce base-load energy and many more jobs as the same investment in coal power.
➢ A ban must be placed on the extraction of coal and other fossil fuels where it involves destructive mountaintop removal.

Oil

Oil spills, whether they occur at the time of exploration, extraction operations, transport or processing, have been the cause of catastrophic pollution. BP, Chevron, Exxon/Mobil, Shell and others have been responsible, and these corporate entities have minimised compensation payments to those adversely affected by the spills.

➢ Action to recover the full taxpayer-funded cost of spills must be taken.
➢ A ban must be placed on the extraction of oil (and other fossil fuels) where it involves deep sea, Arctic and Antarctic drilling.
➢ Though the energy potential of oil sands and shale may be enormous, present technology causes mega-scale environmental damage in the extraction process. Such damaging activity by profit-oriented energy companies

must be immediately stopped and replaced by investment in renewable energy.

Gas

> ➤ The use of gas as an energy source must be closely monitored:

>> - it may involve 'fracking';
>> - if extracted from shale, its effects may be worse than coal for the environment;
>> - if natural gas, its extraction and transport involves major pollution of the environment and frequently the elimination of animal species.

Nuclear

Nuclear power lobbyists claim the technology is now carbon-free.

> ➤ Opponents challenge that argument, its safety and its potential as a basis for a nuclear weapons capability. The 'precautionary principle' (5.1.2) must be applied.

Fracking

Fracking fluids comprise a mixture of water, sand, and hundreds of toxic chemicals and agents, the precise chemical compositions kept secret by the drilling companies.

Though the process may include measures to remove toxic chemicals and agents, a high proportion is left in the ground. The potential to seep into drinking water supplies and nearby aquifers is alarming.

'Fracking' has contributed to subsequent earthquakes.

> ➢ The 'precautionary principle' must be applied: no fracking operations should be permitted until proved safe.
> ➢ Large-scale 'alternative' energy systems such as 'clean coal', 'shale oil' and natural gas obtained by 'fracking' must be replaced as soon as possible by small-scale renewable and sustainable energy systems.

5.2.5. Packaging and Waste

The problem of increasing waste, and its disposal or reuse, arises from consumer lifestyle, globalisation and the worldwide concentration of markets and retail outlets.

Throwaway Mentality—Food, Hard and 'White' Goods

A throwaway mentality has been encouraged by a reduction in the lifespan of goods and the 'manufacture of needs' by corporations.

> ➢ Legislation must be introduced so that corporations and business are held to account not only for their production,

purchasing, labour and advertising practices, but also for their recycling and waste disposal procedures.

➤ Consumers must be persuaded to adopt the attitude 'don't dump it, recycle it'. Details of government recycling facilities must be readily available.

Globalisation and Supermarkets

Globalisation and packaging of goods for transport over long distances, and supermarkets and the display of goods therein have a devastating impact on the environment. Corporate-friendly legislation allows plastic and non-recyclable packaging to be discarded into our oceans and landfill sites.

➤ Enforceable international and national legislation and severe penalties are essential to impose:

- a reduction in market concentration and the prevention of the establishment of unwanted shopping centres and supermarkets;
- the limitation or prohibition of advertising by 'junk mail';
- safe and environmentally friendly packaging (aka 'eco-packaging'), and its recycling or disposal;
- the end of 'shrink wrapping' and plastic bags unless immediately biodegradable;
- environmentally friendly food waste disposal;
- the longest possible useful life for electronic and electrical goods, including computers, phones, televisions, microwave

ovens, and batteries, and their environmentally friendly scrapping and recycling; and

- the disposal or reuse of building and infrastructure construction waste in an environmentally friendly manner.

5.3. Climate Change[29]

5.3.1. Human Impact

Earth's natural systems are complex. The evidence that human activity and the burning of fossil fuels have a major negative impact on the atmosphere and climate change is indisputable and includes:

- rising global average temperatures;
- rapid Arctic and Antarctic ice loss;
- commonplace extreme weather events;
- rising global sea levels;
- increasing fresh water in the Arctic Ocean; and
- reduced European fish size due to warmer waters.

5.3.2. Denial Industry

For decades a global nexus of the 1%, its global corporations and vested interests has deprived the 99% of the will to act on climate change:

- governments have contributed billions in tax concessions and other expenditure to fossil-fuel energy industries;
- the fossil-fuel mining and energy corporations have financed a campaign of denial of human contribution to climate change; and
- a sycophantic academia and mainstream media have joined in the denial.

5.3.3. Action Strategy

Contrary to media assertions, addressing climate change is not a contest between economic 'growth' and the environment. Rather it is an international contest of values and attitudes at all levels of society. As Sir John Houghton stated in *Global Warming: The Complete Briefing*, a coordinated 'war scenario' mentality is required by all to take immediate responsibility for a sustainable future.

➤ By constitutional amendment and legislation, we must immediately:

- consider the economy and a sustainable environment together;
- use international, national and local partnerships and participatory democratic decision-making at all levels to achieve the best social and 'quality of life' outcomes for all communities;
- insist on fair trade (chapter 4) and cooperative endeavour to replace fossil fuels with sustainable renewable energy;

- ensure that action and technologies embrace the concept of localisation, are environmentally friendly and comply with 'precautionary' and 'polluter pays' principles (5.1.2);
- ensure a significant reduction in the rate of loss of our natural world and biological diversity;
- redesign our urban systems and our rural food systems; and
- invest in environmentally friendly public transport infrastructure.

5.3.4. Carbon Emitters Must pay

Carbon Tax: an 'Eco-Tax'

A carbon 'eco-tax' is devised to limit carbon emissions and our use of natural resources such as land, sea and water by making fossil-fuel energy more expensive.

As in all matters economic, the promoters and detractors of a carbon tax operate with widely differing models. Thus their predicted economic outcomes range from 'jeopardising thousands of jobs' to 'creating several hundred thousand sustainable positions'. The latter outcome is prevailing.

Carbon Emissions Trading

Some advocate a market approach, where a carbon tax and its variants and carbon credits/offsets are the preferred market-based trading strategy.

However, eminent persons consider that there is an overwhelming case against a market approach when compared with a tax alone and regulation:

- carbon trading, however disguised, is an untested economic experiment;
- carbon trading favours climate injustice in that it privatises and markets a right to discharge carbon dioxide into the atmosphere;
- corporate market traders and fossil-fuel corporations, disproportionately responsible for carbon emissions, all stand to make windfall profits on increasingly fraudulent 'offset projects'; and
- existing privatised emissions trading schemes don't work, rewarding the worst polluters to carry on as before and to buy cheap 'offset' credits from developing countries.

- ➢ Carbon taxes alone will bring about the needed and vast technological changes to the world's energy system. They are the most direct and most effective way to tackle climate change, far more economically and socially efficient than paying our brightest to develop financial instruments for carbon trading and 'offset credits'.
- ➢ A tax on fossil-fuel energy production at an oil wellhead or refinery is the simplest and most cost-efficient approach.

➤ The following are essential in conjunction with a carbon tax:

- strict and enforced regulation and penalties;
- immediate shifting of subsidies away from fossil fuels to renewables;
- use of carbon tax proceeds to promote investment in renewable environmentally friendly energy sources and the conservation of natural resources; and
- supporting communities already following or pioneering low-carbon ways of life.

5.3.5. Sustainable Renewable Energy Security

Coordinated Action

The existing energy network model requires large centralised base-load fossil-fuel power stations and a grid infrastructure of costly wires and poles connecting them with the areas of electricity demand in cities, towns and industrial areas.

➤ Every nation must ensure the long-term sustainable security of its energy by the development of localised renewable fossil-free and clean energy systems.
➤ Action must be coordinated globally and financed by world organisations and governments, whereby there is:
- immediate public financing of people-owned non-fossil fuel renewable energy systems;
- a moratorium on 'fracking' and new fossil-fuel power plants;

- global institutional ownership of patent right to renewable energy technologies which must be made globally available at minimum cost;
- 'localisation' of manufacturing and agriculture which must be de-industrialised;
- setting compulsory energy-efficiency and carbon emission targets for business;
- the compulsory transformation to environmentally friendly production of cement, iron and steel, ammonia, aluminium and petrochemicals; and
- energy micro-generation of zero or low-carbon heat and power by individuals, small businesses and communities, whose surplus energy can be sold to energy providers.

Base-load Fossil-fuel Energy Redundant

Renewable fossil-free energy systems make fossil-fuel power stations redundant.

➤ Vested corporate interests have delayed the use of solar power for decades. 'Solar' homes, cities and nations must be developed.

➤ Public financing of solar systems is essential, in conjunction with the financing of clean energy such as:

- wind energy systems, used in over 70 countries, where homes and manufacturing plants are powered by their own wind turbines; and

- tidal and wave energy systems—wave power estimated to have a potential energy capability of at least twice the world's current use.

5.4. Urban and Rural Ecosystems[30]

5.4.1. Live Green, Sustainably and Efficiently

We can no longer allow the 1% to destroy our urban and rural ecosystems, the atmosphere in which we live, the air which we breathe, and our flora and fauna.

➢ We must globally live 'green', sustainably and cooperatively rather than competitively. Such 'eco-living' does not involve poverty, but efficiency and environmental wellbeing.

5.4.2. Localisation

More environmentally friendly and efficient localised and durable economies and urban and rural systems are critical for the people to meet their needs.

➢ It is essential that:

- urban and rural systems are self-sufficient, not dependent on long-distance supply, and conform to the realities of a post-carbon era;

- towns and farms conform to smaller, people-orientated, localised and decentralised systems which are self-sustaining within their own land base;
- local democracy and planning by local communities is emphasised;
- desirable local communities are financed by government and peoples' community banks; and
- training in manual skills, for green jobs and lifelong learning and skills is government financed.

5.4.3. Co-Housing Communities: Urban, Suburban, Rural

➤ Co-housing communities, urban, suburban or rural that vary from low-rise structure to town-houses and detached dwellings must be encouraged. Their features adapt to local needs, but generally include:

- developments of 20 to 40 homes which share communal facilities and green space;
- shared common house facilities including larger kitchens, dining rooms, laundries and child care;
- homes looking out on a common garden and built close together, leaving land for shared gardening, recreation or socialising;
- communal pedestrian areas, where children play safely; and
- emphasis on neighbourhood values, such as community choirs, gardening groups, and communal recycling and composting.

5.4.4. Transport

Investment in Public Transport Infrastructure

➢ Publicly owned infrastructure for the transport of people and goods by bus, rail, or boat, and for reallocating freight from heavy duty trucks to rail is essential.

➢ The research and use of alternative non-fossil fuels and the transition to non-commuting work systems must be subsidised by government.

Road

➢ To encourage the use of public transport and shared vehicle use, a 'congestion tax' should be used.

➢ The production and use of the least energy efficient vehicle models must be phased out.

➢ Fuel efficiency standards must be mandated for all new motor vehicles.

➢ Increased vehicle efficiency standards, lighter materials and better aerodynamics to reduce vehicle carbon emissions must be an urgent priority funded by government.

Air

Estimates put aviation's share of carbon emissions and greenhouse gases at about 5 per cent.

➤ Flying taxes, paid by individuals or freight transporters must be introduced.

Ship

➤ The world's marine transport is carbon-based. The use of people-owned 'sails technology' must be financed by government.

Fuel

➤ There are several alternative non-fossil fuel technologies. The development of the best of them must be financed by government and the technology people-owned.

5.5. Urban Systems[31]

5.5.1. City Drift

Unsustainable Cities

The majority of the world's people live in urban areas and cities, where they are packaged into controllable parcels.

The drift to the city from rural areas caused by corporate agribusiness and the creation of needs and advertising by the 1%

is part of the dream of an impossible Utopia (e.g. 'the American dream'). The environmental and social costs of city drift are lives that are dysfunctional, aloof, and often joyless. The costs include:

- infrastructure dominated by the fossilised auto-motive industry, its motorways and bitumen;
- a polluting and energy-intensive process to transport food across and between countries;
- the unsustainable growth of high-rise buildings, megastores and suburbia, normalised by the propaganda of the 1%, yet proven to be increasingly dysfunctional and with a finite future;
- time-consuming commuting to and from work by car, which is stressful and environmentally and socially destructive;
- city pedestrians who have increased their walking speed as they rush from place to place;
- a tripling of the size of our houses, stainless steel appliances, flat screens, and a staggering growth in the number of cars and SUVs;
- a loss of sense of family and community, in which homes, goods and services are bought on credit by debt-ridden and overstressed individuals and two-income families;
- endemic and stressful urban noise including leaf blowers and jet skis; and
- a steep decline of many common bird and other wildlife populations.

5.5.2. Eco-living

Humans and Nature

The notion that cities or material goods or a combination of them can guarantee happiness is an illusion created by the 1%.

Eminent persons assert that embedded in human biology is a deep affiliation with nature—the 'biophilia' hypothesis: when humans are deprived of contact with nature they suffer psychologically and a measurable decline in well-being. Ecologically friendly cities, 'eco-cities', and 'eco-buildings' are designed to overcome the lack of interaction between humans and their natural physical environment.

Eco-Cities

> Cities should be limited to their current land area and infrastructure. Spending on urban infrastructure for private motor vehicles other than the appropriate repair of existing infrastructure must cease.
> Some specific policies are:

- design cities for people—not for motor vehicles—for rail and bus public transport, bicycle pathways and bicycle hire facilities;
- ensure that, where possible, adjustment to public transport infrastructure uses existing roads and rail;

- work towards an urban environment with more people living in less space;
- build liveable suburbs with shared public spaces and developments which do not involve significant infrastructure;
- plan cities to eliminate megastores and urban sprawl and promote small local business;
- place responsibility for sustainable planning in the hands of local communities, financed by people's community banks;
- invest in sustainable urban water and sanitation and clean renewable energy; and
- protect public service broadcasting, museum funding, public libraries, parks and green spaces.

Eco-Buildings

➤ Sustainable 'eco-building' design needs:

- strict government regulation and penalties to ensure minimal energy use and carbon emissions by commercial and public buildings;
- national standards requiring world's best practice in water and energy efficiency standards for all new buildings; and
- a national effort and finance to retrofit homes and encourage investment in clean renewable energy and water efficient homes.

5.5.3. Eco-Towns: Transition Towns

Governments must consider the support and funding of eco-towns and villages, and transition towns.

5.6. Rural Systems[32]

5.6.1. Corporate Agenda: Control and Industrialisation of Agriculture

Agribusiness has vandalised our environment and undermined the basic rights of people and nations. Funded by global financial institutions, global corporations control our food and water supplies, and have taken over:

- our rural and productive lands, dispossessing previously effective small-scale and family farms;
- food production by a system of monopolies favouring genetically modified (GM) seed and mono-crops, and the 'factory farming' of livestock, poultry and fish;
- agricultural inputs such as labour and fertilisers;
- the manufacture of farm plant, machinery and equipment; and
- the distribution and supply of farm products to supermarkets, often through 'home brands', and to fast-food outlets.

The corporate takeover has been on the agenda of the 1% to monopolise world trade in major commodities such as corn, wheat, soy, cotton, and other products. It has required the cooperation of world organisations and governments, and has used:

- a globalised export-oriented agricultural model dominated by a few corporate agribusinesses;
- manipulation of the 'free' trade and investment rules of the WTO, IMF and World Bank, which force countries to favour industrialised agricultural, food and water systems;
- subsidies and the dumping of agricultural products on world markets; and
- massive expenditure on industrialised production, and falling and unsustainable market prices to take over vulnerable small independent farmers.

In doing so they have:

- caused a worldwide and devastating decline in rural jobs and populations, and displaced land owners—rural workers and their families have drifted to urban areas;
- made the transport of commodities to markets responsible for an estimated one-third of greenhouse gas emissions; and
- decimated bird, bee and other wildlife populations by land clearing and polluting fossil-fuel by-products used for pesticides and fertiliser.

5.6.2. Rural Ecosystems: Sustainable Agriculture and Living

➢ To break the corporate agribusiness monopolies, a rapid development of localised smaller and human-orientated rural systems that are self-sustaining is essential. It requires:

- de-industrialisation of agribusiness, the localisation of agriculture, and self-sufficiency by means of small-scale farming;
- import/export controls and government support away from supermarkets towards local food movements and diets that are locally orientated and seasonal;
- technologies that are environmentally friendly, and do not involve unsustainable agribusiness practices, chemical and water over-use and water pollution;
- orderly re-ruralisation, and revitalisation of rural communities and village life by way of land reform, education and the application of eco-agricultural micro-farming methods; and
- strengthening of community-based sustainability initiatives, including the planting of trees and vegetation.

➢ Each one of us must contribute to localisation and the local economy, by making do with less, sharing more, and putting people, the local community and the planet first.

5.6.3. GM Crops

Corporate agribusiness and GM crops have proved an environmental and social disaster. Yet another corporate 'denial' industry is hell-bent on promoting the fear that ecological and organic agriculture is inferior and can only produce low yields from a given land area.

However, sustainable organic agriculture, aquaculture, and aquaponics can meet global food needs:

- in developed countries, yields from ecologically sustainable agriculture are generally comparable to conventional yields;
- in developing countries, ecologically sustainable agriculture practices can greatly increase productivity.

There are now proven alternatives to GM crops, including:

- city farming by its residents,
- 'natural sequence farming',
- the transition to permaculture-based food production, subsidised by government.

LINKS

CHAPTER 1 OCCUPY' GLOBAL ACTION FOR JUSTICE

[1]1.11% WEALTH & CONTROL

http://www.globalresearch.ca/analysis-of-financial-terrorism-in-america/

http://www.informationclearinghouse. info/article29500.htm

http://www.democracynow.org/2011/10/26/glenn_greenwald_on_occupy_wall_ street

http://www.economist.com/node/21543178

http://www.alternet.org/economy/five-ugly-extremes-inequality-america-contrasts-will-drop-your-chin-floor

http://www.alternet.org/story/154745/

http://www.opednews.com/articles/The-plutocrats-who-bankrol-by-Jim-Hightower-120607-152.html

http://www.commondreams.org/view/2012/09/28

http://www.journalof911studies.com/resources/2013McMurtryVol35Feb.pdf

[2]1.2 TODAY'S CRISES

http://www.alternet.org/news-amp-politics/theres-violent-world-war-going-millions-
     casualties-oligarchs-vs-everyone-else

http://www.globalresearch.ca/the-911-plan-cheney-rumsfeld-and-the-continuity-of-government/5320879

http://www.globalresearch.ca/crisis-of-the-u-s-dollar-system/3482

http://www.tomdispatch.com/post/175480/tomgram%3A_barbara_ehrenreich_and_john_
     ehrenreich%2C_the_ fall_of_the_%22liberal_elite%22/#more

http://w3.newsmax.com/a/final_turning/video.cfm

http://www.naomiklein.org/shock-doctrine

http://accadenelmondo.blogspot.com.au/2012/10/fwd-imf-drops-alarming-financial.html

    Martin D. Weiss PhD.

http://us.macmillan.com/static/therealcrash/index.html

http://www.moneyandmarkets.com/19-countries-in-fiscal-trouble-10-in-good-shape-49960

http://www.guardian.co.uk/sustainable-business/rio-20-tim-jackson-leaders-green-economy?newsfeed=true

http://www.salon.com/2012/06/08/apocalypse_soon/singleton/

http://www.commondreams.org/view/2012/08/31

http://www.alternet.org/election-2012/noam-chomsky-fate-humanity-stake-why-are-romney-and-obama-too-cowardly-talk-about-what

[3]1.3 PARTICIPATORY DEMOCRACY & JUSTICE

http://crossingthet.wordpress.com/2008/05/28/can-i-quote-you-st-thomas-aquinas-on-activism-and-anger/

http://en.wikipedia.org/wiki/Occupy_movement

http://occupycorporatism.com/about-us/

http://www.thesolutionsjournal.com/node/1095

http://www.iopsociety.org/

http://www.fightbacknews.org/2012/8/26/sds-completes-southern-tour-preparing-rnc-protests

http://www.alternet.org/147-people-destroying-world

http://www.commondreams.org/ headline/2012/10/30-2

http://www.greenbooks.co.uk/Book/427/Occupy-World-Street.html

http://usliberals.about.com/od/socialsecurity/a/Declaration-Manifesto-Of-Occupy-Wall-Street-Movement.htm

http://www.globalresearch.ca/confronting-the-eu-oligarchy-of-governments-joining-forces-for-another-europe/

http://local.350.org/?akid= 2050.224687.oSNURx&rd=1&

http://dissidentvoice.org/2012/06/game-over-for-the-climate/

http://www.theelders.org/

http://www.witness.org/

http://youthactivismproject.org/

[4]1.4 RESISTANCE TO CHANGE

http://en.wikiquote.org/wiki/Niccol%C3%B2_Machiavelli

http://www.client9themovie.com/

http://www.salon.com/2013/02/12/what_does_a_police_state_look_like/?source=newsletter

http://www.monbiot.com/2013/02/25/corporate-blowback/

http://www.guardian.co.uk/commentisfree/cifamerica/2011/nov/15/occupy-anarchism-gift-democracy

http://www.americanprogress.org/issues/2011/11/ta_111711.html

http://www.alternet.org/story/153972/

http://www.alternet.org/story/154577/

http://rt.com/usa/news/dark-fbi-internet-calea-876/

http://www.alternet.org/story/156466/did_the_nypd_break_international_law_ in_suppressing_protest

http://www.fightbacknews.org/2012/8/2/bond-denied-nato-protester-recharged-after-case-was-dismissed

http://www.globalresearch.ca/how-the-fbi-monitored-the-occupy-movement/5317536

http://www.guardian.co.uk/commentisfree/2012/dec/29/fbi-coordinated-crackdown-occupy

CHAPTER 2 SHAM DEMOCRACIES

[5]2.11% THE ENEMIES OF DEMOCRACY

http://www.globalresearch.ca/it-has-happened-here-in-america-the-police-state-is-real/5322223

http://www.guardian.co.uk/commentisfree/2013/jan/09/bradley-manning-wikileaks-mistreated-progressives

http://www.wired.com/dangerroom/2013/02/54-countries-rendition/

http://www.alternet.org/print/world/inside-bush-administrations-lawless-global-torture-
   regime-and-how-obama-remains-complicit

http://www.informationclearinghouse.info/article34043.htm

http://www.democracynow.org/2013/1/30/ex_cia_agent_whistleblower_john_kiriakou

http://www.alternet.org/story/144529/are_americans_a_broken_people_why_we%27ve_
   stopped_fighting_back_against_the_forces_of_oppression

http://quotes.liberty-tree.ca/quote_blog/David.Rockefeller.Quote.103D

http://ampedstatus.org/exclusive-analysis-of-financial-terrorism-in-america-over-1-million-
   deaths-annually-62-million-people-with-zero-net-worth-as-the-economic-elite-make-
   off-with-46-trillion/#rules

http://www.globalresearch.ca/puppet-state-america/5312360

http://www.globalresearch.ca/index.php?context=va&aid=8450

http://www.salon.com/2008/03/14/superclass/

http://www.alternet.org/story/151999/meet_the_global_financial_elites_
   controlling_%2446_trillion_in_ wealth

http://www.opednews.com/articles/S-P-and-the-Bilderbergers-by-Ellen-Brown-110819-544.html

http://en.wikipedia.org/wiki/Statute_of_limitations

http://en.wikipedia.org/wiki/Double_jeopardy

http://en.wikipedia.org/wiki/Piercing_the_corporate_veil

http://dissidentvoice.org/2011/12/a-death-sentence-for-africa/ (8 key issues)

http://www.monbiot.com/2013/01/14/bang-goes-the-theory/ (neoliberalism)

http://www.onlineopinion.com.au/view.asp?article= 8884&page=0

http://www.wsws.org/en/articles/2010/07/wiki-j30.html

http://www.democracynow.org/2011/10/26/glenn_greenwald_on_occupy_wall_street

http://www.alternet.org/story/156170/glenn_greenwald%3A_how_america%27s_
   surveillance_state_breeds_ conformity_and_fear

http://www.truthdig.com/report/item/state_of_fear_20130107/

http://www.alternet.org/story/156466/did_the_nypd_break_international_law_in_
   suppressing_protest

http://www.alternet.org/environment/police-accused-using-torture-tactics-against-
   nonviolent-keystone-xl-pipeline-protesters

http://johnpilger.com/articles/why-wikileaks-must-be-protected

http://www.abc.net.au/4corners/stories/2012/06/14/3525291.htm

http://www.democracynow.org/2008/7/25/main_core_new_evidence_reveals_top

http://www.salon.com/2012/11/03/why_does_obama_get_a_pass_on_civil_liberties/

http://www.nobelprize.org/nobel_prizes/literature/laureates/2005/pinter-lecture-e.html

http://www.globalresearch.ca/hegemony-and-propaganda-the-importance-of-trivialisation-
    in-cementing-social-control/

http://www.npr.org/blogs/itsallpolitics/2012/10/03/162184983/should-tv-stations-refuse-to-
    air-political-ads-that-make-false-claims

http://news.bbc.co.uk/2/hi/middle_east/3661134.stm

http://rinf.com/alt-news/contributions/western-leaders-are-war-criminals/3188/

http://www. thenation.com/doc/20080707/story

http://archive.org/details/FrancisA.BoyleOnTheCaseAgainstBushAndPotentialWarWithIran

http://www.theglobalist.com/StoryId.aspx?StoryId=3217

http://www.abc.net.au/catalyst/stories/s1625368.htm

http://www.salon.com/2009/05/18/torture_25/

[6]2.2 PARTICIPATORY DEMOCRACY

http://www.monbiot.com/2012/03/12/the-shadow-government/

http://www.gregpalast.com/ballotbandits/7ways-download.pdf

http://www.alecexposed.org/wiki/ALEC_Exposed

http://www.spiegel.de/international/europe/dignity-and-democracy-escaping-the-clutches-of-
    the-financial-markets-a-766518.html

http://www.opednews.com/articles/The-plutocrats-who-bankrol-by-Jim-Hightower-120607-152.html

http://www.ifg.org/programs/plutonomy.html#preview

http://presstv.com/detail/2013/02/16/289184/israeli-ownership-of-us-govt-in-jeopardy/

[7]2.3 STRATEGIC DECISIONS

http://thinkexist.com/quotation/if_you_can-t_explain_it_simply_you_don-t/186838.html

http://direct-democracy.geschichte-schweiz.ch/

http://www.citizen.org/Page.aspx?pid=183

http://www.alternet.org/story/156438/why_only_a_constitution_amendment_can_rescue_
american_democracy

http://www.softimp.com.au/evacs/News%20Items/news26Nov07.html

http://en.wikipedia.org/wiki/Virtual_education

[8]2.4 WAR and THE JUDICIARY

http://www.alternet.org/world/noam-chomsky-gravest-threat-world-peace

http://www.alternet.org/civil-liberties/sleazy-military-contractors-are-crying-foul-over-
drones-they-stand-lose-billions

http://www.democracynow.org/2013/2/27/aclu_blasts_supreme_court_rejection_of

http://www.informationclearinghouse.info/article33583.htm

http://www.globalresearch.ca/the-united-states-promotes-israeli-genocide-against-the-
palestinians-2/5320559

http://www.opednews.com/articles/Carmen-Ortiz-And-Stephen-H-by-Glenn-
Greenwald-130117-203.html

http://www.democracynow.org/2013/2/5/kill_list_exposed_leaked_obama_memo

http://www.alternet.org/civil-liberties/5-ways-president-obama-has-doubled-down-bushs-
most-tragic-mistakes

http://www.globalresearch.ca/terrorism-with-a-human-face-the-history-of-americas-death-
squads/5317564

http://www.commondreams.org/archive/2008/03/17/7735

http://mondoweiss.net/

http://www.globalresearch.ca/provoking-the-enemy-seeking-a-pretext-to-wage-war-on-iran/

http://www.democracynow.org/2012/10/5/on_afghan_war_11th_anniversary_vets

http://www.opednews.com/articles/The-War-on-terror---By-by-Glenn-Greenwald-130105-206.html

http://en.wikipedia.org/wiki/Supreme_Court_of_the_United_States

[9]2.5 WORLD ORGANISATIONS

http://www.un.org/en/aboutun/structure/org_chart.shtml

http://www.actionaid.org/search/apachesolr_search/world%20organisations%20
    international?gids[0]=429

http://www.unglobalcompact.org/AbouttheGC/TheTENPrinciples/index.html

http://www.globalpolicy.org/component/content/article/220-trade/52167-profiting-from-
    injustice.html

http://www.globalresearch.ca/illegal-occupation-of-iraq-us-uk-crimes-against-humanity/5317723

[10]2.6 PUBLIC SECTOR

http://www.salon.com/2012/07/26/protectors_of_wall_street/

http://www.canberra.edu.au/corpgov-aps/pub/IssuesPaperNo.3_AppointmentProcesses_
    Final.pdf

[11]2.7 CORPORATIONS

http://www.policy-network.net/publications/4300/Legislating-for-Responsible-Capitalism

http://www.alternet.org/story/146819/america%27s_ten_most_corrupt_capitalists

http://www.alecexposed.org/wiki/ALEC_Exposed

http://www.alternet.org/story/154745/how_american_corporations_transformed_from_
    producers_to_predators

http://www.alternet.org/story/154746/how_high_ceo_pay_hurts_the_99_percent

http://www.alternet.org/print/story/154873/3_corporate_myths_that_threaten_the_wealth_
    of_the_nation

http://www.huffingtonpost.com/lynn-parramore/capitalisms-dirty-secret_b_1408241.html

http://en.wikipedia.org/wiki/Nationalization#United_States

[12]2.8 LOBBYISTS

http://www.motherjones.com/politics/2010/01/wall-street-big-finance-lobbyists

http://www.opednews.com/articles/Conned-Again-by-Paul-Craig-Roberts-081109-377.html

http://mondoweiss.net/2013/03/scared-silence-defeated.html

[13]2.9 MEDIA

http://www.globalresearch.ca/the-alternative-media-challenges-officialdoms-views/5323701

http://consortiumnews.com/2013/01/15/americas-war-for-reality/

http://www.infowars.com/25-facts-that-the-mainstream-media-doesnt-really-want-to-talk-
about-right-now/

http://www.corporations.org/media/

http://blogs.timesofisrael.com/jews-do-control-the-media/

http://www.informationclearinghouse.info/article31835.htm

http://globalvoicesonline.org/about/

http://www.savetheinternet.com/internet-declaration

[14]2.10 ACADEMIA

http://www.alternet.org/education/how-our-universities-have-been-turned-corporate-
marketing-centers

http://www.salon.com/2012/09/24/bad_science_gets_busted/

http://www.opednews.com/articles/A-Bungling-Fox-in-the-Henh-by-Timothy-
McGettigan-111206-348.html

http://www.motherjones.com/tom-philpott/2012/05/how-agribusiness-dominates-public-ag-research

CHAPTER 3 GLOBAL FINANCIAL CRISIS

[15]3.1 FINANCIAL SECTOR

http://johnquiggin.com/2008/09/08/the-end-of-neoliberalism/

http://www.globalresearch.ca/stock-market-crash-post-mortem-for-milton-friedman/10586

http://www.guardian.co.uk/business/2008/oct/24/economics-creditcrunch-federal-reserve-greenspan

http://www.motherjones.com/politics/2010/01/wall-street-big-finance-lobbyists

http://www.**sony**classics.com/awards-information/**insidejob**_screenplay.pdf

http://w3.newsmax.com/a/final_turning/watch.cfm?PROMO_CODE=EC6E-1 &

http://www.wsws.org/en/articles/2012/03/pers-m06.html

http://www.opednews.com/articles/A-dozen-bankers-are-destro-by-lila-york-120226-957.html

http://www.guardian.co.uk/business/2011/jun/02/goldman-sachs-in-yet-another-scrape

http://www.opednews.com/articles/Libor-Scandal-Reflects-a-C-by-Stephen-Lendman-120707-519.html

http://www.informationclearinghouse.info/article29500.htm

http://www.washingtonsblog.com/2012/08/bankster-fraud-is-not-a-victimless-crime-it-has-driven-100-million-into-poverty-killing-millions.html

http://www.globalresearch.ca/the-real-new-world-order-bankers-taking-over-the-world/5322085

[16]3.2 GLOBAL FINANCIAL INSTITUTIONS & REGULATIONS

http://robertreich.org/post/40027650245

http://www.globalresearch.ca/how-the-fed-could-fix-the-economy-and-why-it-hasnt/5324184

http://goldnews.bullionvault.com/gold_nixon_072720119

http://www.imf.org/external/np/obp/orgcht.htm

http://www.opednews.com/articles/2/The-Banking-system-is-not-by-Ann-Kramer-081024-65.html

http://www.alternet.org/economy/its-interest-stupid-why-bankers-rule-world

http://www.commondreams.org/headline/2012/07/25-6

http://www.wsws.org/en/articles/2009/12/regu-d14.html

http://www.informationclearinghouse.info/article31507.htm

http://www.thenation.com/blog/woman-greenspan-rubin-summers-silenced#

http://www.vanityfair.com/politics/features/2011/11/elizabeth-warren-201111

http://www.wealthdaily.com/articles/global-economy-and-gold/3534

[17]3.3 NATIONAL FINANCIAL INSTITUTIONS

http://www.alternet.org/corporate-accountability-and-workplace/bill-moyers-and-matt-taibbi-everyone-pays-if-banksters-dont

http://www.salon.com/2013/02/08/ban_the_credit_ratings_agencies_partner/

http://www.rollingstone.com/politics/news/secret-and-lies-of-the-bailout-20130104

http://www.nytimes.com/2013/02/04/opinion/krugman-friends-of-fraud.html?_r=1&

http://www.corpwatch.org/article.php?id=15805

http://www.spiegel.de/international/business/concern-over-lack-of-regulation-of-shadow-financial-institutions-a-866763.html

http://www.moneyandmarkets.com/washington-vs-sp-just-the-tip-of-the-iceberg-51450

http://dealbook.nytimes.com/2013/02/04/u-s-and-states-prepare-to-sue-s-p-over-mortgage-ratings/?nl=todaysheadlines&emc=edit_th_20130205

http://www.yesmagazine.org/blogs/david-korten/liberate-america

http://www.yesmagazine.org/blogs/david-korten/10-common-sense-principles-for-a-new-economy

http://www.alternet.org/story/156079/how_the_big_banks_run_the_world_--_at_your_expense

http://www.alternet.org/story/155837/how_wall_street_hustles_america%27s_cities_and_states_out_of_billions

http://www.uq.edu.au/economics/johnquiggin/JournalArticles01/CBAPrivatisation01.html

http://www.wsws.org/en/articles/2012/07/pers-j17.html

http://www.huffingtonpost.com/naomi-klein/real-change-depends-on-st_b_141122.html

http://www.brookings.edu/research/testimony/2011/06/14-too-big-to-fail-barr

http://www.yesmagazine.org/new-economy/7-ways-to-transform-banking

http://www.thenation.com/article/165333/revolution-through-banking#

http://www.onlineopinion.com.au/view.asp?article=8133&page=0

[18]3.4 BRING TO ACCOUNT THOSE RESPONSIBLE FOR FINANCIAL CRISIS

http://www.globalresearch.ca/index.php?context=va&aid=10977

http://www.nytimes.com/2011/11/29/business/judge-rejects-sec-accord-with-citi.
html?pagewanted=all&_r=0

http://www.democracynow.org/2011/10/26/glenn_greenwald_on_occupy_wall_street

http://www.alternet.org/story/149634/

http://www.wsws.org/en/articles/2012/07/pers-j31.html

http://www.commondreams.org/headline/2011/11/28-4

http://www.ourfuture.org/blog-entry/2008114717/stripping-paulson-his-remaining-power-money

http://www.opednews.com/articles/Economics-in-Freefall-by-paul-craig-roberts-100715-530.html

http://www.wsws.org/en/articles/2012/08/pers-a15.html

http://www.alternet.org/story/148882/seriously%2C_jail_the_bankers_or_this_economy_
will_never_fully_recover

http://www.huffingtonpost.com/2011/05/16/foreclosure-fraud-audit-false-claims-act_n_862686.html

http://www.thenation.com/article/160066/credit-rating-hoax

http://www.alternet.org/story/150904/7_ways_hedge_funds_lie%2C_cheat_and_steal

http://ndukeszpersonalfinance.blogspot.com.au/2010/04/big-myth-about-stocks.html

http://online.wsj.com/article/SB10000872396390444024204578044390473058954.html

http://www.economist.com/node/379728

http://www.generationim.com/media/pdf-al-gore-10-05-05-speech.pdf

http://www.investorhome.com/darts.htm

http://www.alternet.org/story/149631/

http://www.cbsnews.com/8301-31727_162-20001981-10391695.html

http://www.publicintegrity.org/accountability/finance/corporate-accountability/whos-
behind-financial-meltdown

http://www.nytimes.com/2011/05/17/business/17bank.html?_r=2&emc=na&

http://www.alternet.org/story/146819/america%27s_ten_most_corrupt_capitalists

http://www.motherjones.com/politics/2011/11/9-wall-street-execs-who-got-off-scot-free

[19]3.5 TAXATION

http://www.monbiot.com/2013/01/21/a-telling-silence/

http://www.yesmagazine.org/issues/what-would-nature-do/inside-the-down-to-earth-
economy? http://www.abc.net.au/am/content/2013/s3682225.htm

http://www.ntu.org/tax-basics/history-of-federal-individual-1.html

http://eslkevin.wordpress.com/2011/06/13/robert-kall-calls-for-reversion-to-taxation-levels-
for-wealthy-at-a-rate-of-eisenhower-through-reagan-era/

http://www.alternet.org/story/151135/

http://www.laclawyers.com.au/document/Taxation-Law-__-Taxation-Disputes-__-Default-
Assessments.aspx

http://www.fpif.org/articles/taxing_financial_speculation_raising_funds_for_critical_needs

http://www.sourcewatch.org/index.php/Financial_transaction_tax

http://inside.org.au/private-gains-and-social-losses/

http://www.alternet.org/story/150367/stop_corporate_tax_cheats%21_u.s._uncut_
movement_goes_global

http://www.hm-treasury.gov.uk/tax_avoidance_gaar.htm

CHAPTER 4 REAL ECONOMY CRISIS

[20]4.1 'REAL' ECONOMY

http://en.wikipedia.org/wiki/Economic_system

http://www.opednews.com/articles/A-Bungling-Fox-in-the-Henh-by-Timothy-
McGettigan-111206-348.html

http://monthlyreview.org/2012/09/01/the-crisis

http://www.unicef.org.au/search.aspx?searchtext=poverty&searchmode=anyword

[21]4.2 ECONOMIC GROWTH v SUSTAINABILITY

http://www.sd-commission.org.uk/pages/links.html

http://www.guardian.co.uk/sustainable-business/rio-20-tim-jackson-leaders-green-
economy?newsfeed=true

http://www.commondreams.org/view/2013/02/25-1

http://www.yesmagazine.org/issues/how-cooperatives-are-driving-the-new-economy/the-cooperative-way

http://www.alternet.org/economy/6-economic-steps-better-life-and-real-prosperity-all

http://www.eurekastreet.com.au/article.aspx?aeid=9135

http://www.opednews.com/articles/Does-Anybody-Else-Think-Ge-by-Dave-Lindorff-081125-537.html

http://www.globalresearch.ca/the-globalization-of-poverty-inside-the-new-world-order/5313987

http://washington.cbslocal.com/2012/11/15/census-u-s-poverty-rate-spikes-nearly-50-million-
americans-affected/

http://en.wikipedia.org/wiki/Gross_domestic_ product

http://www.feasta.org/documents/feastareview/daly.htm

http://www.angelfire.com/pa4/kennedy4/gross.html

http://www.abc.net.au/science/slab/rome/default.htm

http://blogs.ft.com/economistsforum/2008/05/trust-the-development-experts/

http://www.foe.co.uk/community/tools/isew/replace.html

http://www.jri.org.uk/brief/BriefingNo14_4thEdition_July.pdf

http://hdr.undp.org/en/statistics/

http://www.sd-commission.org.uk/publications.php?id=915

²²4.3 GOVERNMENT REVENUE & EXPENDITURE

http://www.globalpost.com/news/business/debt-crisis

http://www.eurekastreet.com.au/article.aspx?aeid=16407

http://webofdebt.wordpress.com/2013/02/13/how-congress-could-fix-its-budget-woes-permanently/

http://www.alternet.org/economy/9-greedy-ceos-trying-shred-safety-net-while-pigging-out-
corporate-welfare

http://www.alternet.org/5-ways-beat-plutocrats

http://www.counterpunch.org/2010/07/23/not-bad-policy-but-class-policy/

http://cpd.org.au/2007/09/deeper-in-debt/

http://www.pbs.org/nationalparks/people/historical/muir/

http://www.opednews.com/articles/The-War-on-terror---By-by-Glenn-Greenwald-130105-206.html

[23]4.4 INDIVIDUAL DEBT

http://cpd.org.au/2007/09/deeper-in-debt/

http://www.tomdispatch.com/post/175643/

http://www.webofdebt.com/

http://www.davidmcwilliams.ie/2009/11/11/forget-the-past-we-must-take-control-of-our-future

[24]4.5 GLOBAL DEREGULATION
(Economic Globalisation)

http://www.tradewatch.org.au/guide/New_WTO_Guide.pdf

http://www.globalresearch.ca/understand-the-globalization-of-poverty-and-the-new-world-order/25371

http://www.greenparty.org.uk/files/reports/2004/Time%20to%20Replace%20Globalisation.html

http://www.gatt.org/trastat_e.html

http://finance.moneyandmarkets.com/reports/event/rwr/one-nation.

php?ccode=0122135442109RWR&em CHINA

http://www.ifg.org/alt_eng.pdf

http://cgt.columbia.edu/files/papers/2005_Overselling_Globalization.pdf

http://en.wikipedia.org/wiki/Monsanto

www.ifg.org/pdf/**Broad**%20**Cavanagh**.pdf

http://www.actionaid.org.uk/100621/blog.html?article=2729

http://news.bbc.co.uk/2/hi/programmes/documentary_archive/7091266.stm

http://www.globalpolicy.org/nations-a-states/state-sovereignty-and-the-global-economy.html

[25]4.6 DOMESTIC DEREGULATION

http://www.informationclearinghouse.info/article29823.htm

http://www.alternet.org/story/87405/squeezing_the_american_dream%3A_workers_face_
    diminishing_returns

http://www.opednews.com/articles/Government-Keeps-Us-Rich-by-Salvatore-Babones-121230-671.html

http://www.alternet.org/economy/6-economic-facts-life-america-allow-rich-run-our-wealth

http://www.alternet.org/story/49540/family_values_begin_at_home%2C_but_who%27s_home

http://labor.net.au/news/1122871084_20333.html

http://www.ilo.org/global/research/global-reports/global-wage-report/2012/WCMS_194843/
    lang--en/index.htm

http://www.abc.net.au/am/content/2010/s3066120.htm

http://www.alternet.org/story/153093/privatization_nightmare%3A_5_public_services_
    that_should_never_be_handed_over_to_greedy_corporations

http://johnpilger.com/articles/in-mexico-a-universal-struggle-against-power-and-forgetting

http://www.smh.com.au/news/arts/architecture-ten-years-on-the-spin-
    cycle/2005/12/15/1134500952335.html?

http://www.uq.edu.au/economics/johnquiggin/JournalArticles02/PrivatisationCEDA02.pdf

http://www.yesmagazine.org/new-economy/a-new-deal-for-local-economies

[26]4.7 POPULATION

http://news.bbc.co.uk/2/hi/science/nature/7865332.stm

http://en.wikipedia.org/wiki/E-borders

CHAPTER 5 ENVIRONMENTAL CRISIS

[27]5.1 POLLUTION & CLIMATE CHANGE

http://news.bbc.co.uk/2/hi/science/nature/3686106.stm

http://www.ipcc.ch/pdf/assessment-report/ar4/wg1/ar4-wg1-frontmatter.pdf

http://www.alternet.org/fracking/5-reasons-natural-gas-wont-be-environmental-and-
    economic-savior

http://www.monbiot.com/2012/12/31/annus-horribilis/

http://www.commondreams.org/headline/2013/01/09-3

http://www.ifg.org/pdf/manifesto.pdf

http://www.corpwatch.org/article.php?id=1048

http://www.sd-commission.org.uk/publications.php?%20id=915

http://understory.ran.org/2011/11/30/as-durban-climate-talks-get-underway-new-report-
highlights-top-bankrollers-of-global-warming/

http://www.jri.org.uk/brief/Briefing_14_3rd_edition.pdf

http://www.alternet.org/story/150997

http://www.acfonline.org.au/news-media/media-release/australians-want-healthy-
environment-and-society-not-just-economic-growth

http://www.globalexchange.org/programs

http://www.thenation.com/article/169089/feel-burn-making-2012-heat-wave-matter#

http://www.feasta.org/2012/12/04/revolution-justified-review/

http://www.worldwatch.org/node/9448

http://www.alternet.org/story/150997/vision%3A_how_to_change_our_laws_so_that_
corporations_don%27t_trump_communities

http://www.ifg.org/programs/plutonomy.html#preview

[285]5.2 POLLUTION

http://en.wikipedia.org/wiki/Rachel_Carson

http://www.abc.net.au/4corners/content/2006/s1754114.htm

http://planetark.org/wen/67960 and http://planetark.org/wen/67590

http://www.yesmagazine.org/issues/what-would-nature-do/four-steps-to-less-wasteful-
communities-zero-waste

http://www.state.gov/j/drl/rls/hrrpt/2010/eap/154398.htm

http://www.alternet.org/story/147528/the_great_pacific_garbage_patch_is_bigger_than_
the_continental_us%3A_here%27s_what_we_can_do_about_it

http://www.dailykos.com/story/2012/01/01/1050579/-The-Dirty-Secret-of-World-Trade-One-
Super-Container-Ship-SO2-Greater-than-50-million-Cars

http://www.publicintegrity.org/node/7900/

http://www.spiegel.de/international/world/our-ravaged-seas-globalization-is-destroying-the-world-s-oceans-a-570877-3.html

http://www.unep.org/geo/geo4/report/05_Biodiversity.pdf

http://www.sciencedaily.com/releases/2008/12/081215091017.htm

http://www.enn.com/top_stories/article/44078

http://ecowatch.org/2012/grandmother-demands/

http://www.circleofblue.org/waternews/2012/world/national-security-assessment-water-scarcity-disrupting-u-s-and-three-continents/

http://www.alternet.org/story/154648/5_deadly_threats_to_our_precious_drinking_water_supply

http://www.rain-tree.com/facts.htm

http://www.ran.org/forests

http://www.conservation.org/about/pages/about_us.aspx

http://uk.reuters.com/article/2007/02/07/uk-environment-crime-eu-idUKL0790850020070207

http://www.alternet.org/story/125783/

http://www.popularmechanics.com/science/energy/coal-oil-gas/biggest-oil-spills-in-history#slide-1

http://www.truthdig.com/report/item/20090526_chevron_shell_and_the_true_cost_of_oil/

http://www.alternet.org/story/148794/

http://www.citizen.org/fracking-unsafe-unregulated

http://www.alternet.org/story/153467/the_fracking_industry_has_bought_off_congress%3A_here_are_the_worst_offenders

http://europa.eu/rapid/press-release_SPEECH-12-900_en.htm

http://www.dailymail.co.uk/news/article-2075942/Stores-told-cut-packaging-year--face-crackdown.html

http://www.recyclingnearyou.com.au/

http://www.guardian.co.uk/environment/2012/sep/21/england-carrier-bag-charge-poll

[29]5.3 CLIMATE CHANGE

http://www.thenation.com/article/why-we-cant-wait#

http://www.abc.net.au/science/slab/rome/default.htm

http://planetark.org/wen/67520

http://www.sustainable.unimelb.edu.au/content/pages/post-carbon-pathways

http://reneweconomy.com.au/2013/deutsche-sees-sustainable-global-solar-market-in-2014

http://www.alternet.org/environment/myth-human-progress

http://www.alternet.org/environment/how-country-one-worlds-largest-economies-ditching-
fossil-fuels

http://www.greenleft.org.au/node/34586

http://www.dailykos.com/story/2011/12/05/1042444/-The-Most-Important-News-Story-of-
the-Day-Millennium

http://www.commondreams.org/headline/2012/08/28-0

http://www.informationclearinghouse.info/article32572.htm

http://www.spinwatch.org/reviews-mainmenu-24/book-reviews-mainmenu-23/5314-
newspeak-in-the-21st-century-by-david-edwards-and-david-cromwell-media-lens

http://www.monbiot.com/2011/12/08/a-levelling/

http://www.sierraclub.ca/national/programs/atmosphere-energy/nuclear-free/index.shtml

http://www.jamesrobertson.com/news-dec06.htm#stern

http://e360.yale.edu/feature/putting_a_price_on_carbon_an_emissions_cap_or_a_tax/2148/

http://www.world.org/weo/environment

http://local.350.org/?akid=2050.224687.oSNURx&rd=1&t=1

http://reneweconomy.com.au/2012/in-a-renewable-world-baseload-generation-is-redundant-21817

http://reneweconomy.com.au/2012/future-of-fossil-fuels-back-up-for-renewables-99836

http://en.wikipedia.org/wiki/Microgeneration#Government_policy

http://reneweconomy.com.au/2012/time-to-radically-reform-our-energy-system-says-iea-18671

http://www.abc.net.au/rural/telegraph/content/2012/s3488758.htm

[30]5.4 URBAN AND RURAL ECOSYSTEMS

http://reneweconomy.com.au/2013/why-consumers-wont-need-the-power-industry-any-
more-53948

http://www.globalpossibilities.org/back-to-the-land-again-folk-schools-teach-skills-for-
modern-day-survival-2/

http://greenparty.org.uk/files/reports/2004/LIVE%20local%20shops%20and%20high%20
streets.htm

http://www.carolinelucasmep.org.uk/2002/12/16/look-to-the-local/

http://www.earth-policy.org/about_epi/6/

http://www.sd-commission.org.uk/publications.php?id=915

http://www.yesmagazine.org/issues/the-new-economy/31-ways-to-jump-start-the-local-economy

http://www.yesmagazine.org/new-economy/money-that-works-for-local-communities

http://www.independent.co.uk/property/house-and-home/come-together-could-communal-
living-be-the-solution-to-our-housing-crisis-6260020.html

http://www.globalexchange.org/news/climate-change-activists-drop-20-foot-banner-
challenging-toyotas-eco-hypocrisy-ny-auto-show

http://www.unep.org/newscentre/default.aspx?DocumentID=2694&ArticleID=9266

http://www.guardian.co.uk/sustainable-business/full-transition-sustainable-economy-
forces?INTCMP=SRCH

http://en.wikipedia.org/wiki/The_Bed_of_Nails_(Yes_Minister)

[31]5.5 URBAN SYSTEMS

http://www.opednews.com/articles/JESUS-OF-SUBURBIA-by-Jim-Quinn-090513-119.html

http://www.alternet.org/economy/after-ruining-america-era-giant-chain-stores-over

http://en.wikipedia.org/wiki/Sustainable_city

http://biophiliccities.org/biophiliccities.html

http://kunstler.com/blog/2013/01/some-sunny-day.html

http://www.acfonline.org.au/be-informed/sustainable-living/creating-sustainable-cities

http://www.alternet.org/story/148794/don%27t_give_up%3A_sierra_club_leader_on_how_
we_can_win_the_fight_for_clean_energy

http://www.nabers.com.au/page.aspx?code=ABOUTUS&site=1

http://www.climatechange.gov.au/en/climate-change/fifth-assessment/factsheet.aspx

http://biomimicryinstitute.org/case-studies/case-studies/termite-inspired-air-conditioning.html

http://en.wikipedia.org/wiki/Eco-towns

http://en.wikipedia.org/wiki/Transition_Towns

[32]5.6 RURAL SYSTEMS

http://www.foodandwaterwatch.org/reports/the-economic-cost-of-food-monopolies/

http://www.actionaid.org.uk/_content/documents/power_hungry.pdf

http://en.wikipedia.org/wiki/Food_sovereignty

http://oaklandinstitute.org/node/2572

http://en.wikipedia.org/wiki/Natural_Sequence_Farming

http://www.earthpolicy.org/index.php?/book_bytes/2009/pb4ch09_ss5